knitting for
radical self-care

knitting

for

radical

self-care

A MODERN GUIDE

BRANDI CHEYENNE HARPER

ABRAMS, NEW YORK

contents

PART I

radical self-care

7   getting powerfully, daringly free

13   the principles

PART II

a modern guide to knitting

19   the framework

19   adventurous beginning knitting

33   casting on and binding off for modern edges

46   all about shaping and construction

60   finishing like a boss

65   simple stitches

PART III

patterns

74   tombolo cowl

84   allay jacket

92   sojourn shawl

100   dawn cowl

108   joie mittens

116   ode cardigan

128   audre cowl

136   sola scarf

140   aura cowl

144   terran hat

151   *the land*

154   *muses and earth angels*

156   *about the author*

158   *index*

PART I

radical self-care

getting powerfully, daringly free

2020

The J train is humming quietly in the background, the nightly fireworks light the air, the streets whistle with diverse, masked faces chanting "Black Lives Matter." This is a time of unrest, of a great unlearning. Racism, the patriarchy, heteronormativity, the gender binary are systems of inequality designed to disconnect us from each other, from our hope, creativity, and power. We must dismantle them brick by brick for every generation, past and future. Love and determination are the connective threads woven through each of our communities as we work to change laws, redistribute funds, and invest at the grassroot level to create equity among us. We are strong, growing, learning, and searching as we become powerfully, daringly free.

unlearning

Angela Davis says, "Radical simply means grasping things at the root." As I write this book about my craft, I am also actively acknowledging and unpacking the ways white supremacy and capitalism contribute to my lack of self-worth and inclination to burn out. Always being of service, taking care of my body last, and accepting less than what I am worth are some of the lessons I am unlearning. Finding refuge in my own ability to design the life I want to live is the most powerful tool I have acquired in my liberation. Revisiting the writings of Audre Lorde during this time in my life has been a blessing. And her work around guilt was the first lesson I needed in order to begin the process of owning my power and honoring myself without hesitation. Guilt was a barrier obstructing my growth; I felt guilty when I took days off to rest, when I said no to someone, for what I did not know about myself and my history. "Guilt is not a response to anger," Lorde said. "It is a response to one's own actions or lack of action. If it leads to change then it can be useful, since it is then no longer guilt but the beginning of knowledge. Yet all too often, guilt is just another name . . . for defensive destruction of communication; it becomes a device to protect ignorance and the continuation of things the way they are, the ultimate protection for changelessness." Guilt has been useful. I no longer feel guilty for what I did not know, for what I am only now learning, and the ways I have abandoned myself for others. And what I'm learning is ushering me into this profound place of knowing and trusting in my innate ability to empower myself and manufacture the tools to empower another.

celebrating black women

I am Black, of African ancestry. A Black woman. A Black knitter. A Black queer. A Black woman who loves Black women. Toni Morrison declared, "If there is a book you want to read, you're going to have to write it yourself." I want to share the story of a little Black girl, fourteen and ambitious, who taught herself to crochet, inspired by her grandmother's afghans. Who managed yarn shops owned by people of color from high school through college, trading paychecks for merino wool. Black women are few and far between in the history lessons I learned in school. Morrison, thank goodness, was among them. I hope a little Black girl learning to make her own clothes will pick up this book one day and see herself represented in the pages. This book pays homage to my revolutionary ancestors and living peers who advocate for their freedom so we can do the same.

my values

The self-care values I'm exploring within this book and within my own life in this present moment are creativity, authenticity, and courage.

Creativity keeps me purposeful. It taps me into my gut. I wake up excited for the day ahead. Creativity takes me off the bench, watching my life pass me by, and gets me into the game, calling plays and making moves. When I am supporting my creativity, the future feels hopeful and blessings feel abundant. Some of my most inspiring design ideas and crafty business solutions reveal

themselves when I'm sweeping the floor, sautéing a green vegetable with garlic, stretching my hips, bending my spine, separating my knitting supplies by type, or moving through a workday after eight full hours of sleep. When I consciously make decisions that support my physical and spiritual health, my body becomes a site for liberation and limitless creativity. When I am exhausted, nutrient deficient, with chores piling up, depression can wash over me like a murky wave. My ideas feel stupid, I isolate myself, I don't want to knit, I feel powerless, and I become deeply fearful of my own success. Creativity is hard work and takes so much discipline. I write lists every day, make routines, and then change them. But engaging in my creativity is an active part of my own self-care. Self-care is not about fixing all of our problems or knitting all day. For me, it is the daily practice of returning to the place where I believe I can make anything, be anything I set my mind to. It only requires that I try. My hope is that we can begin to see the ways creativity feeds our self-care and to share my own tools for keeping my creativity alive.

Who am I? What brings me happiness? Who can love the whole of me? Taking the very best care of myself requires getting to know myself better, seeking out people who mirror the life I am living and want to live, under-standing my socialization. We learn to sit in straight lines for hours at a time, memorizing without comprehension. We are taught to wear all kinds of masks under the guise of professionalism, to fit in and to protect ourselves. I remember my grandmother telling me, "You skin your teeth too much. Young girls shouldn't skin their teeth too much." This is Jamaican patois for smiling a lot. I was eight or nine years old at the time. I realized much later in life this was her way of trying to shield me, a young girl, in a world that equates kindness with weakness, optimism with naivete. Being authentic for me means putting my joy on display, telling a friend I am sad, asking for help and not pretending I have it all figured out. I hope sharing myself fully empowers you to do the same.

"WHEN I DARE TO BE POWERFUL—TO USE MY STRENGTH IN THE SERVICE OF MY VISION, THEN IT BECOMES LESS AND LESS IMPORTANT WHETHER I AM AFRAID."

—Audre Lorde

Creativity really does take courage. It's like jumping off a cliff into a body of water; it can make your heart beat a little faster. I often feel fear putting my work into the world; there is this moment of hesitation. It becomes easier over time with every vulnerable moment.

I'm rooting for you.

I'm rooting for me.

the principles

When I speak of radical self-care, I'm speaking of the transformative shift we make in our perspectives. Inquisitive dialogue inside quiet solitude. How we show up in and for our communities. How we actualize our potential. Connecting and surrounding ourselves with nature. Radical self-care is a collection of the actionable steps we take to manifest our values in our day-to-day lives.

Each pattern's essay is rooted in the following eight self-care principles, all an exploration of how to love ourselves and each other a little deeper in the context of making.

intersectionality

Making things sometimes means having access to certain communities, access to resources, access to tools, access to time, access to space. When we lack access to the things we want, this can affect our self-worth. Creativity becomes a luxury for those who feel welcome, who have enough time, who have enough money. If we are to empower ourselves, our companies, our communities, we must first acknowledge how the interconnected nature of race, class, gender, sexuality, disability, age, and appearance can limit access to our creativity and to creative spaces. Our knitting experiences can be impacted by our literacy, the color of our skin, how much money we have, how much we weigh, our gender, or our physical ability.

Some people have limited access to knitting and knitting communities because of a disability. I am seemingly able-bodied, but chronic stress and inflammation exacerbate my perennial allergies to dust, mold, pet dander, and industrial chemicals. My skin responds by getting so dry and cracked I cannot move my hands to knit. My natural lifestyle is filled with organic whole foods to nourish my body, plants to clean the air, botanical products to hydrate my skin, asanas to manage my stress, and prescribed medication as a consistent line of defense. All in an effort to keep doing this work of tapping into my potential as a hand-made designer and guide.

When the viral conversations broke out about racism and the lack of diversity and representation within the knitting community, some questioned what skin color even had to do with knitting. For many, the connection was clear. As a Black teenage knitter, I was often ignored or suspiciously monitored in yarn shops, an awareness many Black people, regardless of economic status, know well. Folks of all ethnicities email me with sweet messages just to acknowledge what seeing a Black knitter on Instagram means. Representation does matter.

Knitting is a craft that requires tools and materials, so I understand continuous exploration can be cost-prohibitive for those with limited expendable income. Sometimes we have to go a little farther, search a little longer, work a little harder to access what enables us to practice self-care. That journey is worth it. My family lived in inner-city projects while I was growing up—eight people in a three-bedroom apartment. My mother rose at 5 a.m. every day. She would get us ready for school, then work as a nurse for eight hours a day before coming home to make dinner and help us with our homework. Some of her self-care practices are making playlists, sitting alone in her car and not driving, just lip-syncing to gospel music. She was in the kitchen when I asked her for money once as a kid to buy a ball of yarn. "Ten dollars for a ball of yarn?! That can put food on someone's table for a week," she said. "Brandi, you need to get yourself a job." One year later, when I was sixteen, I landed my first job at a yarn shop.

I recognize that I am privileged in identifying with the gender I was assigned at birth, having a college degree, being light skinned, and appearing seemingly able-bodied and straight-passing. I am also underserved for having grown up under the poverty line in an anti-Black world as well as being openly gay and femme. Having access to knitting as a form of self-care is both a privilege and a right. I share many of my personal experiences within this book through this lens of intersectionality, relating them to my craft to contribute to our collective learning and help continue the vital conversations we as a society are having.

make mistakes

After twenty years as a knitter, I still make mistakes: forget an increase, drop a stitch to realize inches later, twist my round, skip the needle change, or miss a row repeat. Learning to knit harnesses courage, commitment, and a willingness to mess up. Knitters are resilient. So many mistakes in my life I will never be able to go back and fix. Knitting is a soft place to land. *Fudging* is another word for being flexible. Don't worry, you'll make a way.

identifying challenges

What can the art of knitting teach us about the real world as we navigate being human? While learning how to throw pottery on the wheel, I noticed I was prone to holding my breath. Centering the clay, a process of moving every particle in the same direction, seemed nearly impossible. But with deep breaths, the clay steadily spun without a wiggle. When my hands snagged the clay, causing the whole structure to collapse, my teacher instructed me to use more water. And when I rushed for time's sake, hours of pots leaped to the ground, over-crowded on the drying board. Steady breathing, staying hydrated, slowing down, and not overextending are challenges I also notice within my knitting practice. Sometimes I have to put the knitting down and make a cup of tea or stretch into downward dog. Sometimes, I have to say no to another design collaboration, remind myself I am not missing out, and return to unfinished projects.

What are the three things that challenge you most in knitting? My hope is you'll find tools, words, and a path to overcoming these challenges within your own creative practices as we move through this book together.

striving for simplicity

My inclination has always been to do the most. Cables! Lace! Crochet accents! Colorwork! Now, let's combine them all! As my wardrobe and home design style became more minimal and ethically sourced, I found myself with dozens of projects I never wore. Just before casting on for this book, I had this idea to design an elaborate high-waisted skirt with a petticoat. My ego was hard at work to prove myself to the world. Would I wear the skirt, ever? Maybe once for the 'gram. Where am I going to store this huge wired underskirt? In one of my few NYC-apartment-sized closets? I scrapped the idea with a few others in place of wearable knits we can reach for every day, all the time, and make again and again.

The entire book is very much a physical and energetic clearing of what is superfluous in my design practice, in my home, of what I make to feed my ego and prove I am worthy of the recognition my work receives, what drains my bank account, what keeps me jumping from place to place trying to be everything to everyone, what I overconsume to not feel my emotions. The colors I wear, the art I collect, right down to my teapot and ironing board, have been edited to soft colors, pastels, and neutral tones. I want to create a tiny universe for us filled with uncomplicated fabrics, warm and practical, made of animal fibers dyed in soothing colors using plants. My ultimate goal is to create simple patterns that are intricately constructed.

striking a balance

Knitting induces a seductive sense of completion. It can also be a form of distraction, an act of escapism. When I deprive myself of rest, I'm more prone to make mistakes. I can knit to the point where other areas of life begin unraveling at the seams. Or I may complete so many tasks on my list, but none is a row of knitting. Our job is to find balance. I have yet to perfect bringing all the pieces of my life together such that the joining points are invisible from the outside and the seams impeccable. Balance sometimes means putting the yarn down. Sometimes it means picking it up.

reading the work

Reading your knitting is being able to look at your fabric and know what it is you've done and what it is you'll be doing next. This skill often shows up in patterns as "knit your knits and purl your purls" or "work as established." Once we set the foundation, we understand where to go from there. I love this kind of standardized reinforcement we can apply to everyday life, a reminder that *we got this*. That once we have a little direction, we know where to go. Reading

the work allows us to be more independent. Look back at a row and see the knit two together, the yarn-over increase. Trust the pattern. Trust yourself.

mindfulness in practice

Every knit stitch is a tiny meditation. To welcome the full benefits, knit in silence and without technology. Have tea with your thoughts. Knitting is a vehicle in which to evolve our consciousness and craft the life we want to live. Ground yourself in this present moment.

adventurous beginner mind

You can own the title of adventurous beginner from day one of your knitting journey. You can be an experienced knitter for half your life and still be an adventurous beginner. This book will ask you to try alternative ways of creating techniques already familiar to you. Frolic in learning with the light-heartedness of a child running in a meadow.

PART II
a modern guide to knitting

the framework

Let's level up!* The Modern Guide to Knitting framework is my approach to
knitting and includes all you need to know to make the patterns in this book.
This chapter covers every stitch, technique, and abbreviation used. We'll dive
into teaching you the basics of knitting if you don't already know or need
a refresher. Techniques range from beginner to experienced, and I've orga-
nized them into four sections. Together, the Adventurous Beginning Knitting;
Casting On and Binding Off for Modern Edges; All About Shaping and Construction; and Finishing Like a Boss sections are my way of creating modern,
skillfully constructed handmade knitwear. Be gentle with yourselves as you
learn a new skill or an alternative way of doing something already familiar to
you. Once you know how to begin and complete a knitted square, you are all
set. Before diving into the patterns, be sure to check out the sections on yarn
and essential tools, reading my patterns, abbreviations, gauge, and the simple
stitches I think are perfect for a minimal, modern style.

adventurous beginning knitting

If you are completely new to knitting and you've picked up this book to learn
how to knit, welcome! It's about to get so lit; this entire framework will be like
a wild ride full of excitement. Learn even a handful of the techniques laid out
in this chapter and you'll feel like a rock star. This section guides you through
a quick lesson on how to get stitches on your needles, the Knit Stitch, the
Purl Stitch, and how to get stitches off your needles. There are two styles of

---

* "Level up, level up, level up, level up," Ciara sings. "You know you want this yummy, yummy
  all in your tummy!"

19

knitting: one where you hold your working yarn with your left hand, another where you hold your working yarn with your right. I use both methods, depending on what I'm making and who I'm teaching, and both create stitches that look the same. Here, I show you how to knit holding the yarn with your right hand.

To get started, get yourself:

- One skein of bulky weight yarn. I'm using Purl Soho "Wooly Wool" (100% wool; 109 yards/200 grams) in Peach Lily, or choose another light color you like
- 24" circular needles size US 15 [10 mm]
- A large-eye tapestry needle for weaving in loose ends
- A pair of scissors

Learn the following four techniques to make your first knitted square. We'll cover abbreviations later in this chapter. For now, just know RH means right-hand and LH means left-hand. If you're feeling really adventurous, you can turn your practice piece into a long, chunky scarf. You got this!

basic knit cast on

Step 1: Make a slipknot by looping the yarn into a pretzel shape, leaving an 8" [20 cm] tail hanging along the right side. (Photo 1)

Step 2: Slip the knitting needle under the strand at the center right of the pretzel. (Photo 2)

Step 3: Pull the yarn ends apart to tighten the loop on your needle. This counts as your first cast on stitch! (Photo 3)

Step 4: Hold the needle with the loop in your LH. Pick up the other needle with your RH and insert it into the loop from front to back, crossing the RH needle behind your LH needle. Pick up the yarn with your RH (Photo 4)

Step 5: Wrap the yarn behind and around your LH needle. (Photo 5)

Step 6: Bring your RH needle forward, guiding the yarn under and through the loop. (Photo 6)

Step 7: Pull a loop onto your RH needle. Now you have one loop on each side. (Photo 7)

Step 8: Secure the loop on your LH needle with your thumb and place the new loop from your RH needle onto your LH needle. (Photos 8 and 9)

You've casted on your first stitch! Repeat Steps 4 to 8 until you have 20 cast on stitches or your desired number of stitches. Each loop counts as one stitch.

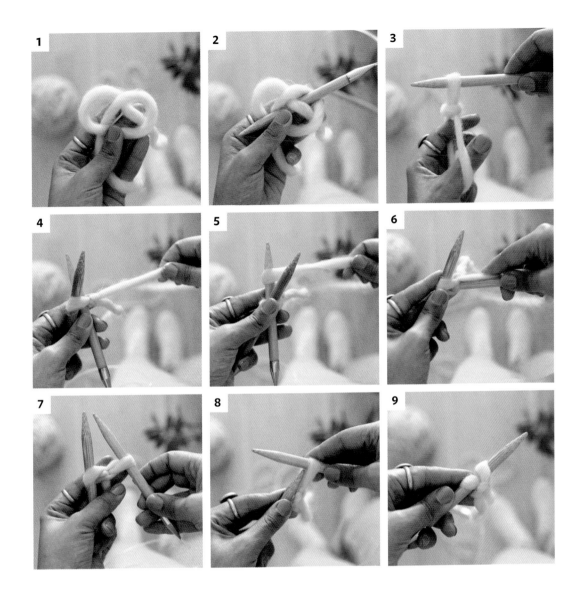

the knit stitch

Step 1: Always make sure your stitches are facing down in the same direction before you start a new row and begin knitting your stitches. (Photo 1)

Step 2: With the yarn behind your needles, insert your RH needle into the first loop from front to back, crossing the RH needle behind your LH needle. (Photo 2)

Step 3: Wrap the yarn behind and around your LH needle, as you did in Steps 4 and 5 of the Basic Knit Cast On, and bring your RH needle forward, guiding the yarn under and through the loop. (Photo 3)

Step 4: Pull a loop onto your RH needle. (Photo 4)

Step 5: Now drop the first stitch you just went through off the LH needle. Yes, just drop it like it's hot! Sometimes, you'll have to push the stitch up from below so the first one can come off easily; just be gentle. You did it. You've just knit your first stitch! A knit stitch looks like a V. (Photo 5)

Step 6: Repeat Steps 1 to 5 until you've knit all your stitches. (Photo 6)

To work your next row, simply switch hands so your stitches are in your LH and the working yarn is coming from the first stitch on your needle. On the back side of knit stitches, you'll see small bumps at the bottoms of your stitches. This is the last row you've made, and what purl stitches look like. Go ahead and practice the knit stitch until you feel comfortable with the technique, knitting all your stitches every row to create what is called Garter Stitch (page 66). Then you're all set to learn the purl stitch!

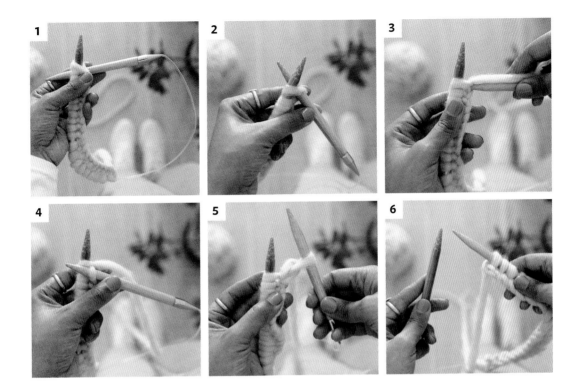

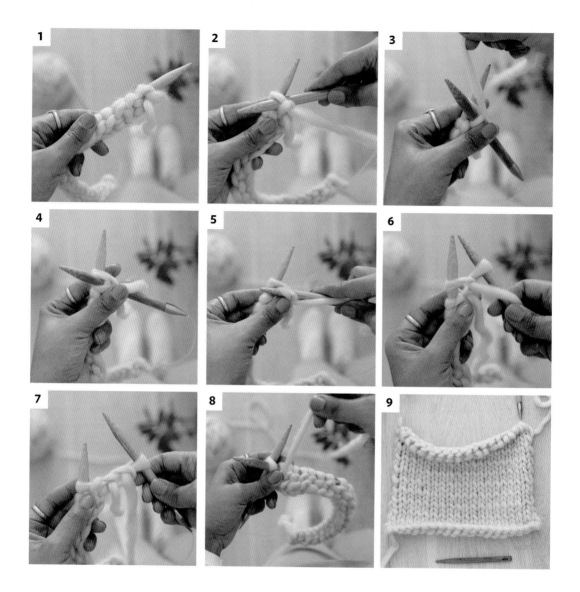

the purl stitch

Step 1: Always make sure your stitches are facing down in the same position before starting a new row and beginning to purl your stitches. (Photo 1)

Step 2: With your yarn in front, insert your RH needle from back to front and down into the first stitch on your needle. (Photo 2)

Step 3: Using your RH, wrap the yarn between your two needles. (Photo 3)

Step 4: Bring the yarn forward and to the right, creating an open loop on your RH needle. (Photo 4)

Step 5: Guide your RH needle back, bringing the yarn under and through the stitch. (Photo 5)

Step 6: Pull a loop onto your RH needle. (Photo 6)

Step 7: Now, drop the first stitch you just went through off the LH needle, securing your new stich with your RH index finger so the stitch doesn't fall off. You've just purled your first stitch! A purl stitch has a little bump. (Photo 7)

Step 8: Repeat Steps 2 to 7 until you've purled all your stitches. Secure your last stitch with your LH thumb. If it does fall off (and it's bound to happen), simply put it back on your LH needle and complete your row. (Photo 8)

Go ahead and practice purling by alternating one knit row and one purl row for Stockinette Stitch (page 66). Work back and forth until you feel comfortable with both the knit and the purl stitch, ending with a purl row. You can make a nice size scarf with just one ball of Purl Soho "Woolly Wool," and I say go for it! Stockinette is one of the very few stitches I think looks beautiful without a finished, more involved edge. The edges will roll toward the purl side, and it looks cool. Or knit a small square like I did. Just be sure to save enough yarn to bind off all your stitches. You need a tail three times the width of the piece you'll be binding off. If your piece is 10" [25.5 cm] wide, then you'll need about 30" [76 cm] of tail. (Photo 9)

basic knit bind off

Step 1: Knit 2 stitches onto your RH needle. Note: you can also purl 2 stitches, or knit 1 stitch, then purl 1 stitch, depending on your stitch pattern and the instructions you're following. Here we will knit all of our stitches as we bind off. You need 2 stitches on your LH needle to bind off 1 stitch. (Photo 1)

Step 2: Insert your LH needle in front of the first stitch on the needle from left to right. (Photo 2)

Step 3: Pull the first stitch over the second stitch and over the tip of the RH needle, bringing the first stitch onto your LH needle. (Photo 3)

Step 4: Now drop the first stitch off your LH needle. You just bound off your first stitch! (Photo 4)

Step 5: Knit 1 stitch, so you have 2 stitches on your RH needle. (Photo 5)

Step 6: Repeat Steps 2 to 5 until all your stitches are bound off and one loop remains on your RH needle. To finish, cut an 8" [20 cm] tail and pull the loop up and out to fasten it off. No need to add any knots! (Photo 6)

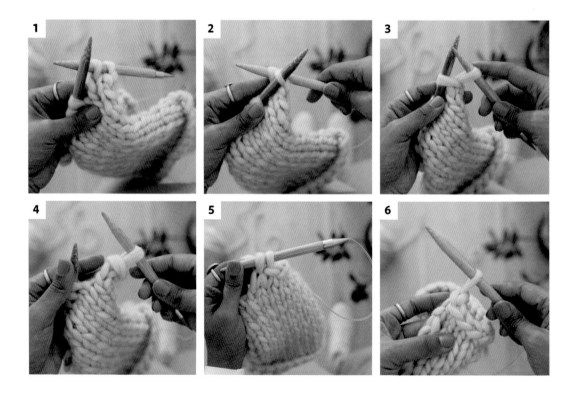

weaving in ends

Step 1: Thread your tail through your tapestry needle. Flip the work over to the wrong side, or the side you see being most hidden when worn. (Photo 1)

Step 2: There are many ways to weave in your ends such that the tail is nearly invisible on the other side of the fabric. I'm showing you just one way. The key is to insert your tapestry needle under the strand of yarn between 2 stitches. Sometimes you'll have to look at the other side of the work to know you are actually between 2 stitches. A knit stitch is easier to identify; it looks like a V. You want to go under the strand just next to that V. Weave the needle into the strand between 2 stitches on a diagonal across the work. Weave in your ends at least 2" [5.5 cm] deep. (Photo 2)

Step 3: Now, to secure the tail, turn and weave the end back in the other direction. (Photo 3)

Step 4: No need to add any knots! Just cut the tail, leaving a little extra yarn at the end. Your ends will be almost invisible on the other side. (Photo 4)

Whenever you have to join a new ball of yarn, simply drop the old yarn and begin knitting with the new ball, leaving an 8" [20 cm] tail. Maybe there's a hole or two, maybe you have more stitches than you started with; maybe you threw the knitting across the room and went to find snacks; maybe your piece looks exactly like mine. There is no wrong way to begin. You did it!

yarn and essential tools

I discovered merino wool at age fifteen and fell in love. It stands up well after seasons of washing, steaming, and stretching. It's gentle enough for those with an itchy wool sensitivity. I encourage you to substitute the suggested materials with yarn from your favorite shops. Use plant-based materials, fiber blends, and budget-friendly yarns. Shop local, support independent dyers and spinners, and seek ethically made yarns from socially conscious companies whenever accessible. I am deeply grateful to Ocean Rose of Ocean by the Sea, who sourced and botanically dyed the merino I used in some of the projects in the book. She uses materials like walnuts, soaked rice, and other vegetables to create deep earth tones. She works with natural protein fibers produced ethically with non-mulesing practices.

Many of my patterns require several different needle sizes and notions. You'll acquire more essential tools like double pointed needles (dpns) for hats, mittens, and sleeves; circular needles with various lengths; different kinds of stitch markers and crochet hooks. Changing needle sizes is such an easy way to create knits that look intricate and filled with depth. All the tools you need to make your piece will be listed in the materials section of each pattern.

pattern reading

I like the words *established* and *begin*, the phrases *as follows* and *once again*. I decided to get rid of some standard abbreviations within the patterns themselves. My hope is you'll be able to read through each essay and pattern with ease by spelling more of the terms out. You'll find stitches as *stitches*, not *sts*, and *remaining* instead of *rem*. Some phrases, like *slip 1, knit 2 together, pass slipped stitch over*, do need to be abbreviated to *sk2p*. Foundation rows are for placing markers and setting up a stitch pattern. Whenever possible, I like for right-side rows to land on odd-numbered rows.

You will be instructed to insert your needle into a stitch *knitwise* or *purlwise*, *as if to knit* or *as if to purl*. Knitwise, or as if to knit, means inserting your needle up into the stitch from front to back, crossing the right-hand needle behind the left-handle needle as if you're going to knit. Purlwise, or as if to purl, means inserting your needle down into the stitch from back to front, crossing the right-hand needle in front of the left-hand needle as if you're going to purl. I'll also say *knit your knits and purl your purls*. This means when you see a knit stitch, what looks like a V, you knit it. When you see a purl stitch, what looks like a little bump, you purl it.

There is a term in knitting called *fudging*. This means do what you have to do to make it work and look nice. There is no road map except the one you create in the moment. Do you really need to rip back 3 inches, or can you just knit two stitches together right here and now to get back to the correct stitch count in such a way that not even you would notice? If so, then fudge it.

These are my favorite knitting terms and symbols:

[ ] work instructions within brackets as many times as instructed

* repeat the instructions following the asterisk as instructed

" inch(es)

Find all abbreviations used on page 32.

checking your beloved gauge*

Check my gauge.
Check my gauge.
I'll make a swatch and check my gauge.
I made a swatch and checked my gauge.
I did it. I did it!
I washed it and blocked it!
I do it. I did it.
I promise I'll do it.

I wrote that little jingle just for you. Read it out loud. Let it be a mantra, a lesson, a tool before every project. Use it as you wish, but whatever you do, check your dearly beloved gauge. Here is what happens when I don't.

It tripled in size. My first pattern for *Vogue Knitting*, the Fitted Dress, took a month to design, make, and write. I checked my gauge per inch over Stockinette Stitch, but the skirt section was knit in Garter. I didn't wash the swatch. I didn't block it. I was running around buying yarn and holiday supplies, selling knitwear, proofreading the dress pattern during my lunch breaks at my forty-hour-a-week job. Curbing sleep and cutting corners. I was making it happen, doing big things fueled by passion and filled with purpose. Too often, though, I chose speed over focus, quantity over quality. Like all my knits, I dunked the dress in cool water—and a knee-length dress became a wedding dress with a train. I feverishly knit another, adjusting the pattern in three days and three nights to meet my deadline.

Cutting corners almost always ensures I'll end up taking the long way round. The most basic and fundamental aspect of my work, the one thing guaranteeing me ease, fell completely off my list. It's ironic that as I took on more and more, it was my own gauge, an instrument for measuring how much something holds, that was the one thing I neglected.

To ensure you get a finished project similar to mine when knitting one of the patterns in the book, you'll want to match the gauge in the pattern. I recommend taking your gauge this way:

---

* This is a performance piece, do you see?

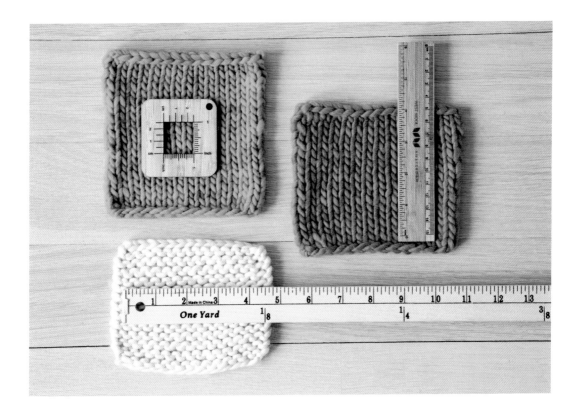

- Measure how many stitches and rows you're getting over 4" [10 cm].

- Double-check the gauge by measuring over 1" [2.5 cm] and then over 2" [5 cm].

If you knit tighter or looser than me, you'll need to adjust your needle size, or possibly your yarn, until you find the right combination that matches the pattern gauge and gives you a fabric you like. I hear a collective sigh from knitters in my classes anytime the word *gauge* is mentioned. Is it a coincidence that another word for gauge is *tension*? I get it, believe me. Still, checking gauge saves time and ensures a proper fit. DO IT. Let's think about gauge as a beloved and treasured step in our knitting practice. Fake it till you make it.

abbreviations

This list includes all the abbreviations used in this book.

APPROX. approximately

BO bind off

BRK brioche knit (see page 69)

BRKYOBRK BRK, yo, BRK into the same stitch (see page 69)

BRP brioche purl (see page 69)

BYO backward yarn over (see page 48)

C6B cable 6 back (see page 71)

C6F cable 6 front (see page 71)

CC contrast color

CN cable needle

CO cast on

DPN(S) double pointed needle(s)

K knit

K2TOG knit 2 together (see page 49)

KFB knit into the front and back of the stitch (see page 49)

KPK knit 1, pick up purl bump, knit 2 together (see page 52)

LH left hand

LLI left lifted increase (see page 47)

M1L make 1 left (see page 46)

M1R make 1 right (see page 46)

P purl

P2TOG purl 2 together (see page 49)

P3TOG purl 3 together (see P2TOG on page 49)

PM place marker

PSSO pass the slipped stitch over

RH right hand

RLI right lifted increase (see page 47)

RS right side(s)

SL slip

SKP slip 1, knit 1, pass the slipped stitch over (see page 50)

SKPP slip 1, knit 1, pass the slipped stitch over, slide stitch back to LH needle, pass second stitch on LH needle over skp (see page 50)

S2KP slip 2 stitches one at a time knitwise, knit 1, pass the 2 slipped stitches over (see page 51)

SL1YO slip 1 with yarn over (see page 69)

SLM slip marker

T&S turn and slip (see page 51)

TBL through back loop

W&T wrap and turn (see page 53)

WS wrong side(s)

WYIB with yarn in back

WYIF with yarn in front

YO yarn over (see page 48)

casting on and binding off for modern edges

casting on

I use several different kinds of cast on methods in my work, depending on the stitch pattern, if I plan to add an edge after the fact, or to establish a specific kind of hem or edge.

LONG TAIL CAST ON

The Long Tail Cast On creates a sturdy, elastic edge. To decrease even the slightest bulk at the cast on edge, let's learn this cast on without making a beginning slipknot. To begin, measure 3 times the width of the piece you are planning to make. For a 4" [10 cm] swatch, you'll need about 12" [30.5 cm] of tail.

Step 1: Position the tail end behind the needle, the ball yarn in the front, grasping the ball yarn and the tail with your left hand. Secure an open loop on the needle with your right index finger. (Photo 1)

Step 2: With the tip of the needle, pick up the front strand from front to back, sliding the needle up your thumb. (Photo 2)

Step 3: With your right hand, bring the needle behind the yarn on your index finger. (Photo 3)

Step 4: Bring the needle down and through the loop on your thumb, allowing the loop to pass over the tip of the needle. (Photo 4)

Step 5: Slip your thumb out of the loop, reposition your thumb behind the front strand of yarn, and gently pull both strands to tighten the stitch on the needle. (Photo 5)

Repeat Steps 2 to 5 for desired number of stitches.

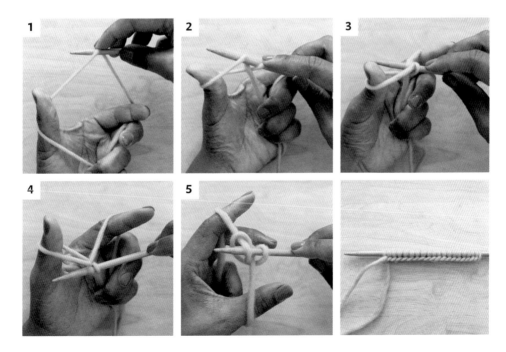

LONG TAIL TUBULAR CAST ON

The Long Tail Tubular Cast On is worth the effort. This cast on creates a p1, k1 border and looks great when followed by any of the simple stitches in this book. It's #1 on my list of techniques all knitters should know. It's fun, challenging, and creates a sense of accomplishment every time. I watched videos many times before committing it to memory. First, we're going to get an odd number of stitches onto the needle in a p1, k1 pattern beginning and ending with a purl stitch. This step is followed by two foundation rows where you knit the knits and slip the purls. You can adjust these instructions so that you begin and end with a knit stitch or cast on an even number of stitches. I recommend using a needle two sizes smaller than the needle you plan to use for the main body to prevent flaring. To begin, measure 3 times the width of the piece you are planning to make.

Step 1: Position the tail end behind the needle, the ball yarn in the front, grasping the ball yarn and the tail with your left hand. Secure an open loop on the needle with your right index finger. This first loop counts as the first purl stitch. (Photo 1)

Make a knit stitch
Step 2: Bring the needle from front to back and under the yarn coming off your thumb. (Photo 2)

Step 3: Bring the needle behind the yarn on your index finger. (Photo 3)

Step 4: To complete the knit stitch, bring the needle forward and under the yarn of your thumb. (Photo 4)

Make a purl stitch
Step 5: Bring the needle behind the yarn on your index finger. (Photo 5)

continues

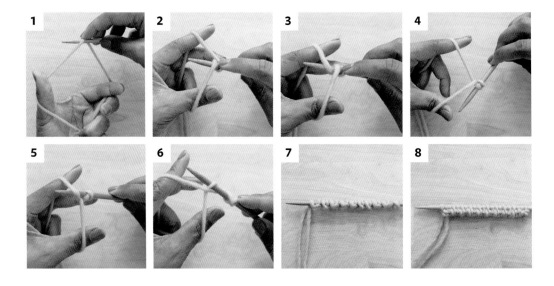

Step 6: Bring the needle in front and under the yarn coming from your thumb, and then under the yarn coming from your index finger. (Photo 6)

Repeat Steps 2 to 6 for desired number of stitches, ending with Step 6.

Foundation Row 1: *k1tbl, slip 1 purlwise wyif; repeat from * to last stitch, end k1. (Photo 7)

Foundation Row 2: slip 1 knitwise wyib, [k1, slip 1 purlwise wyif] to last 2 stitches, k2. (Photo 8)

The first and last stitches of the foundation rows can be worked differently to set up desired selvedge edge.

DOUBLE KNIT EDGE

The Double Knit Edge creates a two-layer Stockinette fabric with a rounded edge. This cast on looks great when worked for 1 to 1½" [2.5–4 cm]. I've added a Stockinette Stitch selvedge edge here. To begin, cast on any number of stitches and work Steps 1 through 6 and Foundation Row 1 of Long Tail Tubular Cast On. Then work Rows 1 and 2 below.

Row 1: p1, *k1, slip 1 purlwise wyif; repeat from * to last 2 stitches, k1, p1.

Row 2: *k1, slip 1 purlwise wyif; repeat from * to last stitch, k1.

Repeat Rows 1 and 2 three more times.

CROCHET CHAIN PROVISIONAL CAST ON

The Crochet Chain Provisional Cast On is worked with a crochet hook and can be used as a decorative cast on that forms a tidy braided edge or as a provisional cast on.

Step 1: Using scrap yarn, make a slipknot (see page 20) and place snugly on crochet hook. (Photo 1)

Step 2: To make a chain stitch, wrap yarn around the hook from back to front and pull a loop through. Chain specified number of CO stitches plus 2 extra and fasten off. (Photo 2)

Step 3: With main yarn and knitting needle, begin at the slipknot end. Insert needle into the back loop of the first crochet chain from front to back, wrap yarn around, and pull a loop through onto needle. Continue to pick up and knit 1 stitch into the back loop of each crochet chain for the specified number of stitches. (Photo 3)

Step 4: Work the pattern as instructed. To free live stitches, gently undo the last chain from the crochet chain. (Photo 4)

Step 5: To secure the live stitches and prevent unraveling, insert a spare needle into the loop below the crochet chain edge from back to front purlwise. Then pull the scrap yarn to free the live stitch above. After releasing the first live stitch, simply pull the tail of the crochet chain to remove the scrap yarn and release the remaining live stitches, placing them on the needle as you go. (Photo 5)

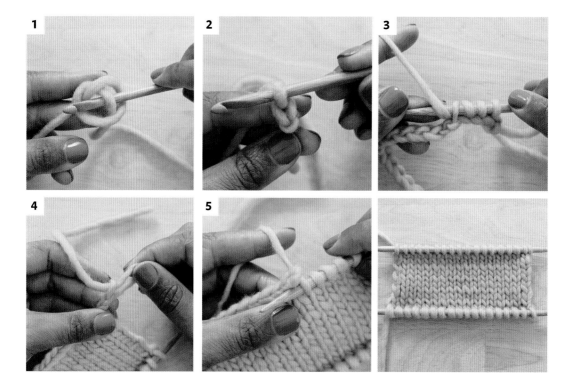

KNIT HEM

The Knit Hem is perfect if you want a thick, double-layered fabric. It's wonderful on the brims of hats and sleeve cuffs.

Step 1: Begin with the Crochet Chain Provisional Cast On (see page 36). Work Stockinette Stitch, beginning with a purl row, until the piece is double the desired length of the hem. Remove the scrap yarn from the cast on edge and place the live stitches on a spare needle.

Step 2: Fold hem in half so the purl sides are facing each other.

Step 3: Insert a needle into the next stitch on the front and back needles at the same time. Wrap the yarn around the needle to knit. (Photos 1 and 2)

Step 4: Knit 2 together to make one stitch on the RH needle, dropping the stitches just worked off the LH needle. (Photos 3 and 4)

Repeat Steps 3 and 4 until all hem stitches are joined.

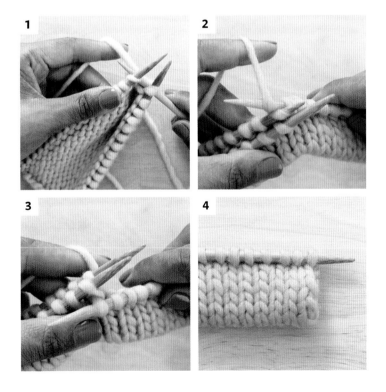

I-CORD CAST ON

The I-Cord Cast On is one of my favorite trimming techniques. There are variations on how this cast on is made. This tutorial lays out how to seamlessly transition from the I-Cord Cast On into an I-Cord Selvedge. You'll make an I-Cord with as many rows as you need stitches, plus 2 rows. For example, when you work an I-Cord for 22 rows, you will only pick up and knit (or purl) 20 stitches across the cord. When you remove the scrap yarn from the provisional cast on, it releases live stitches; those 3 stitches are placed on the needle for the selvedge edge.

Make I-Cord

Step 1: Using the Crochet Chain Provisional Cast On (page 36) and dpns, cast on 3 stitches. (Photo 1)

Step 2: Slide the stitches to the other end of the needle with RS facing. Without turning the needle, place the needle in your left hand. Pulling the yarn from behind, knit the 3 stitches. Pull the yarn snug when knitting the first stitch to neaten the I-Cord joining point. (Photo 2)

Step 3: Repeat Step 2 for as many rows as specified in the pattern. (Photo 3)

Pick up stitches along the I-Cord

Step 4: Slip the 3 working stitches onto a longer needle. Pick up and knit into the top half of the first stitch of each row along the I-Cord. (Photos 4 and 5)

Step 5: Carefully remove the scrap yarn from the provisional cast on. (Photos 6 and 7)

Step 6: Slip the 3 live stitches onto the RH needle with the purl side facing you and working yarn in front. (Photo 8)

This I-Cord Cast On method sets you up to flow effortlessly into a built-in I-Cord Selvedge (page 39).

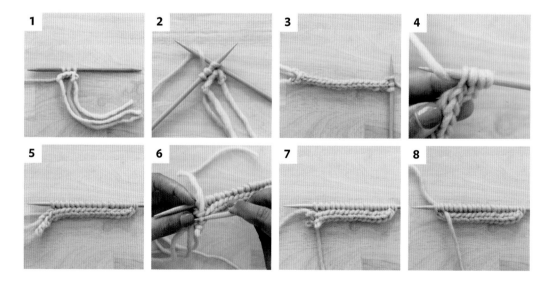

THUMB CAST ON

The Thumb Cast On is not designed to be sturdy. I use this technique to cast on stitches to an existing piece for thumb gussets and collar construction. I always pick up stitches or add an applied edge along this cast on. It's great because it doesn't create a bulky seam. Be careful when you work the first row; the stitches are loose loops around the needle and fall off easily.

Step 1: Hold your working needle in your right hand. Bring your working yarn over your left thumb and index finger, securing the yarn with your other three fingers. (Photo 1)

Step 2: Bring the needle from behind and under the yarn between your thumb and index finger, making a loop on your RH needle. (Photo 2)

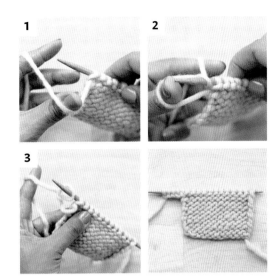

Step 3: Pull the yarn taut to tighten the loop around your needle. (Photo 3)

Repeat Steps 1 to 3 for the desired number of stitches.

selvedges and other edges

These selvedges and edging techniques are a way to get rid of your raggedy edges!

I-CORD SELVEDGE

The I-Cord Selvedge is built right into the fabric—no need to add a neat edge after the fact. This selvedge looks best with 2 to 4 stitches on each side. I love 3 stitches to maintain that nice rounded edge.

To add an I-Cord Selvedge: k3, work pattern to last 3 stitches, slip 3 purlwise wyif. Repeat this row for the I-Cord Selvedge, bringing the yarn behind and pulling the first stitch taut at the beginning of each row.

APPLIED I-CORD EDGE

The Applied I-Cord Edge is the perfect afterthought technique you can add to neaten the edge of a finished garment and keep your knitting flat. I recommend casting on 3 stitches for your I-Cord and using dpns 1 to 2 sizes smaller than the one you used for the main body. Attach the I-Cord with the WS facing. This way, the first 2 or 3 stitches knit in the I-Cord curl neatly to the RS. The key to attaching an I-Cord to any edge is to pick up and knit into the same space along that edge. Pick up into the top half of a selvedge edge or into the center of each stitch along a bind off or cast on edge.

Step 1: Cast on the number of I-Cord stitches called for in the pattern using your preferred CO method. Without turning the work, place the needle in your left hand and slide the stitches to the other end of the needle. Pulling the yarn from behind, k2, slip 1 stitch knitwise wyib from the LH to RH needle. (Photo 1)

Step 2: Insert the needle into the next space along the edge of the main piece and knit into the space. (Photos 2 and 3)

Step 3: Pass the slipped stitch over. (Photo 4)

Step 4: Slide the stitches from one end of the needle to the other without turning. Pull the yarn from behind and k2, slip last stitch knitwise wyib. (Photo 5)

Repeat Steps 2 to 4 until the edge is completely finished with the I-Cord. To fasten off, cut 8" [20 cm] of tail, weave it through the remaining 3 stitches, and pull taut.

REVERSE SINGLE CROCHET EDGING

Reverse Single Crochet is also known as Crab Stitch. This edge is worked from left to right to create a strong cord-like afterthought finish. Reverse Single Crochet looks beautiful on both sides.

Step 1: Insert the hook from front to back into the center of a stitch along the edge and pull a stitch onto the hook. (Photo 1)

Step 2: Insert the hook into the next stitch to the right, grab the yarn with the hook, and draw through a stitch. The 2nd stitch you make will be the first stitch on the hook. (Photos 2 and 3)

Step 3: Pull the yarn through both stitches on the hook. (Photo 4)

Repeat Steps 2 and 3 across the edge. (Photo 5)

To fasten off, cut 8" [20 cm] and pull the last loop up and out.

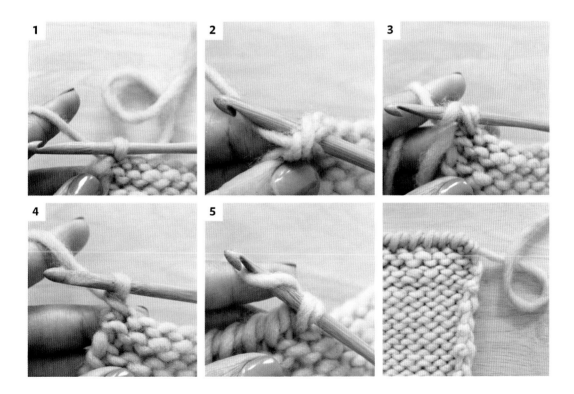

binding off

CROCHET BIND OFF

This bind off uses a crochet hook to replicate the mechanics of the Basic Knit Bind Off. I find it's faster. Instead of slipping 1 stitch over another to bind off a stitch, we pull 1 stitch through another instead. When binding off with multiple strands together, a crochet hook is especially useful and helps create more uniform stitches along your final edge. Use a crochet hook the same metric measurement as your knitting needle or the hook size specified in the pattern.

Step 1: With your crochet hook in your right hand, knit 2 stitches off your LH knitting needle onto the crochet hook. You need 2 stitches to bind off 1 stitch.

Step 2: Use the crochet hook to draw the 1st stitch closest to the hook through the 2nd stitch to bind off 1 stitch.

Repeat Steps 1 and 2 until all stitches are bound off. Cut 8" [20 cm] of tail and pull the last loop up and out to fasten off.

3-NEEDLE BIND OFF

The 3-Needle Bind Off is both a bind off and a seam. It joins together live stitches from two pieces. Using a crochet hook makes for a quicker and more uniform finish.

To begin, position the two pieces so the RS are facing each other, and the needles are parallel.

Step 1: Insert a crochet hook into the first stitch on the front needle, then the first stitch on the back needle at the same time.

continues

Wrap the yarn around the crochet hook knitwise and draw a loop through both stitches, dropping the stitches off each needle. There will be 1 stitch on the hook. (Photo 1)

Step 2: Repeat Step 1 so there are 2 stitches on the hook. (Photo 2)

Step 3: Pull the first stitch through the second stitch on the hook to bind off 1 stitch.

Repeat Steps 2 and 3 until all the stitches are bound off. Cut 8" [20 cm] of tail and pull the last loop through to fasten off.

I-CORD BIND OFF

An I-Cord Bind Off creates a clean, straight edge with little elasticity. This tutorial shows how to seamlessly transition from a 3-stitch I-Cord Selvedge into the bind off. I recommend ending with a RS row and working this bind off with the WS of the fabric facing.

Step 1: Bring the working yarn behind the 3-stitch I-Cord Selvedge. (Photo 1)

Step 2: Knit 2, slip 1 knitwise wyib. (Photo 2)

Step 3: Knit 1 from LH to RH needle. (Photo 3)

Step 4: Pass the slipped stitch over. (Photo 4)

Step 5: Slip 3 stitches from the RH needle to LH needle purlwise. (Photo 5)

Repeat Steps 2 to 5 to the last 3 stitches.

Slip the last 3 stitches to a dpn and turn the work so the working yarn is coming from the back needle and the purl sides of the I-Cord Selvedge stitches are facing each other. Join 3 stitches on each side together using Kitchener Stitch (page 63).

TUBULAR BIND OFF

The Tubular Bind Off complements the Long Tail Tubular Cast On and works great over 1x1 Rib or Brioche. There's no need to work any foundation rows. I prefer binding off with the RS facing. The first stitch must be a knit stitch. Go ahead and purl the last 2 stitches together on the last row if necessary. Cut a tail 4 times the width of the piece to be bound off and thread it onto a tapestry needle.

Step 1: Insert the tapestry needle into the first stitch (it's a knit stitch) purlwise and drop the stitch off the needle. (Photo 1)

Step 2: Insert the tapestry needle into the next stitch (it's a purl stitch) knitwise and pull the yarn through, leaving the stitch on the needle. (Photo 2)

Step 3: Insert tapestry needle from right to left into the left half of the last knit stitch, then into the next knit stitch as if to purl. (Photo 3)

Pull yarn through, keeping the purl and knit stitches on the needle.

Step 4: Insert tapestry needle into first stitch (it's a purl stitch) purlwise, drop both the purl and the knit stitches from LH needle and pull yarn though. (Photo 4)

Repeat Steps 2 to 4 until all stitches are bound off.

The key to a successful Tubular Bind Off is:
- You have to go into each stitch twice before it's officially bound off.

- When you first insert the tapestry needle into a knit stitch, it will always be purlwise. The second time into the same knit stitch will always be knit-wise, before dropping it off the needle.

- You will always insert the tapestry needle into a purl stitch knitwise the first time through and then always purlwise before dropping it off.

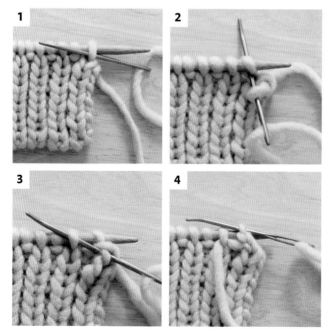

KNIT HEM BIND OFF

The Knit Hem Bind Off creates a double Stockinette Stitch edge. To begin, work Stockinette Stitch until you have double the length you want your hem to be, ending with a knit row. Measure and cut a seaming tail 3 times the width of the hem and thread it onto a tapestry needle.

Step 1: Using a contrasting-color yarn smaller than your main yarn and tapestry needle, weave a lifeline along the row where you'll join the live stitches. A lifeline is a length of yarn woven into your existing fabric to help you easily identify your sewing line. With practice and an experienced eye, you'll be able to eyeball the sewing line along the body of the work without this marker. (Photo 1)

Step 2: With the WS of the work facing you, insert the tapestry needle from below into the first purl bump of the sewing line, just above the lifeline you've placed. (Photo 2)

Step 3: Insert the tapestry needle knitwise into the first stitch on the needle and pull the yarn through. (Photo 3)

Step 4: Drop the stitch off the needle and pull the yarn taut. Let the fabric fold in half. (Photo 4)

Step 5: Repeat Steps 2 and 3 until all live stitches are joined to the sewing line. (Photo 5)

Remove the lifeline and gently stretch the bind off to remove any excess sewing tail. You want to pull the yarn just taut enough to join the live stitches to the fabric, but not so tight the fabric buckles. The joining seam will be nearly invisible on the RS.

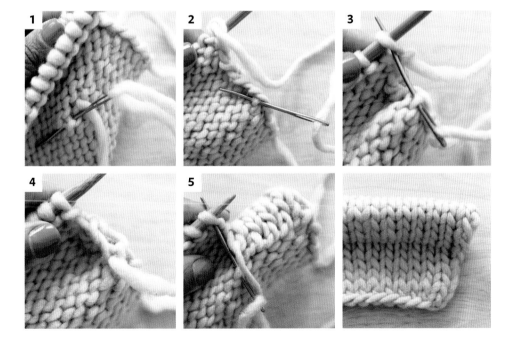

all about shaping and construction

Directional decreases and increases are all kinds of special. They create their own decorative patterns and pull and lift the fabric in interesting ways while also shaping them. Slant them left! Slant them right! As frustrating as it can be, some supposedly complementary decreases—that is, the left-leaning version of a right-leaning increase or decrease—sometimes do not mirror each other exactly. Each technique has its own flavor.

increases

M1R

Make 1 right, a one-stitch increase. Make 1 happen between two stitches. They can tighten up neighboring stitches.

Step 1: Insert the LH needle from back to front under the bar between the last stitch you knit and the next one.

Step 2: Knit into the front of this stitch.

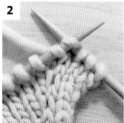

M1L

Make 1 left, a one-stitch increase.

Step 1: Insert the LH needle from front to back under the bar between the last stitch you knit and the next one.

Step 2: Knit into the back of this stitch.

LLI

Left lifted increase, a 1-stitch increase. Lifted increases bloom from an existing stitch. Increasing into that same stitch repeatedly forms a well-defined line.

Step 1: Knit to the stitch where you'll make the increase.

Step 2: Knit the stitch for the increase from the LH needle to RH needle.

Step 3: Insert the LH needle into the left leg of the stitch 2 rows below from back to front and lift the leg onto the LH needle.

Step 4: Knit the lifted stitch through the back loop.

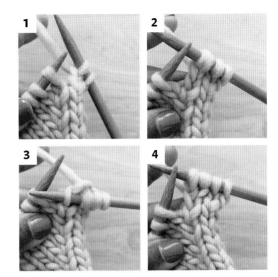

RLI

Right-lifted increase, a 1-stitch increase.

Step 1: Knit to the stitch where you'll make the increase.

Step 2: Insert the RH needle into the right leg of the stitch 1 row below and lift it onto the LH needle.

Step 3: Knit the lifted stitch, keeping the existing stitch on the needle.

Step 4: Knit the existing stitch.

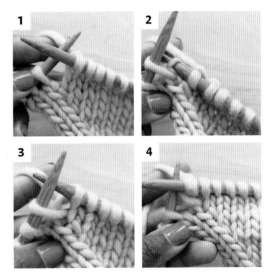

YO

Yarn over, a left-leaning 1-stitch increase. Yarn overs happen between two stitches. They are used to make eyelets in lace patterns, where a decrease is paired with each yarn over to maintain a consistent stitch count. Here we make a yarn over and then close the eyelet it creates to increase our stitch count.

Step 1: Work to the location where you'll make the increase. Bring the working yarn to the front of the work between the needles. Wrap the yarn over the RH needle knitwise.

Step 2: Knit or purl the next stitch to secure the yarn over.

Step 3: On the following row, knit or purl through the back loop of the yarn over to close the eyelet.

BYO

Backward yarn over, a right-leaning 1-stitch increase.

Step 1: Work to the location where you'll make the increase. Bring the working yarn over your RH needle and to the back of the work between the needles.

Step 2: Knit or purl the next stitch to secure the yarn over.

Step 3: On the following row, knit or purl through the front loop of the yarn over to close the eyelet.

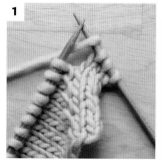
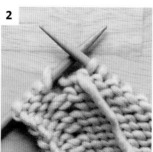

KFB

Knit front and back, a 1-stitch increase. The increase is worked into an existing stitch and creates a little bump resembling a purl stitch.

Step 1: Knit 1 stitch and do not drop the stitch off the LH needle.

Step 2: Bring your RH needle into the back of your stitch and knit it, letting both stitches drop off the LH needle.

decreases

K2TOG

Knit 2 together, a right-leaning 1-stitch decrease. For a right-leaning 2-stitch decrease, you can knit 3 together (k3tog) in the same fashion.

Insert the RH needle into the next 2 (or 3) stitches as if to knit at the same time. Knit the 2 (or 3) stitches together and let them drop off the LH needle.

P2TOG

Purl 2 together, a right-leaning 1-stitch decrease. For a right-leaning 2-stitch decrease, you can purl 3 together in the same fashion. This decrease looks the same as k2tog on the other side.

Insert the RH needle into the next 2 (or 3) stitches as if to purl at the same time. Purl the 2 (or 3) stitches together and let them drop off the LH needle.

SKP

Slip 1, knit 1, pass the slipped stitch over, a left-leaning 1-stitch decrease. For a left-leaning 2-stitch decrease, you can slip 1, knit 2 together, pass slipped stitch over (sk2p) in the same fashion.

Step 1: Slip 1 knitwise wyib.

Step 2: Knit 1 stitch.

Step 3: Insert the LH needle into the slipped stitch, pull the slipped stitch over the k1, and let it drop over the tip of the RH needle.

Use the tip of a dpn to readjust and neaten each skp along the decrease line as needed.

SKPP

Slip 1, knit 1, pass the slipped stitch over (skp), pass next stitch over skp, a right-leaning 2-stitch decrease.

Step 1: Skp, then slip the skp from the RH needle to the LH needle purlwise. (Photo 1)

Step 2: Insert the tip of the RH needle into the 2nd stitch on the LH needle, pull this stitch over the skp, and let it drop off the needle. (Photo 2)

Step 3: Slip the 1st stitch on LH needle to RH needle purlwise. (Photo 3)

S2KP

Slip 2, knit 1, pass 2 slipped stitches over, a centered 2-stitch decrease. A s2kp pulls the fabric inward, forming a slight point.

Step 1: Insert the LH needle into the next 2 stitches at the same time as if to k2tog, and slip these stitches to the RH needle. (Photos 1 and 2)

Step 2: Knit 1 stitch. Insert the LH needle into the 2 slipped stitches, pull the slipped stitches over the k1, and let them drop over the tip of the RH needle. (Photo 3)

short rows

Short rows allow us to work only part of a row. Working a short row wrap or a double stitch eliminates the gaps created when the work is turned. Short rows are perfect for constructing a better fit around the head and neck when shaping collars, hats, and hoods. The end result is that one side, or section, has more rows than another section. When you reach the end point of a short row, patterns will usually tell you to "wrap and turn." This means that you wrap a stitch with the working yarn, turn your work, and continue in the opposite direction. The wrap is worked later to help fill the gap that this creates, making the short rows almost invisible.

GARTER SHORT ROWS

When working short rows in Garter Stitch, you will work T&S (turn and slip 1 knitwise wyib) while creating the short rows, and then KPK (knit 1, pick up purl bump, knit 2 together) to close up the gaps when the short rows are complete.

T&S

Step 1: Work to the stitch specified in the pattern. (Photo 1)

Step 2: Turn to work in the other direction. Slip the first stitch on the LH needle knitwise wyib, pulling the stitch taut on the RH needle. (Photo 2)

Repeat Steps 1 and 2 as directed in the pattern.

continues

KPK

Step 3: Work to the stitch specified in your pattern and knit 1. Insert the tip of your LH needle under the purl bump at the edge of the turning stitch. To close the short-row gap, knit the 2nd stitch on the LH needle together with the purl bump. (Photos 3 and 4)

Repeat Step 3 as directed in the pattern.

GERMAN SHORT ROWS

When working German Short Rows, you will work a double stitch while creating the short rows, and then work those double stitches as a single stitch to close the gaps. German Short Rows are great for short rows in Brioche Stitch.

Make double stitch

Step 1: Work to the stitch specified in your pattern. (Photo 1)

Step 2: Turn the work so the WS is facing. Bring the yarn to the front and over the top of the RH needle. This creates what looks like 2 stitches instead of 1 and looks similar to a sl1yo used in Brioche. (Photo 2)

Repeat Steps 1 and 2 as directed in the pattern.

Step 3: There's no need to close gaps when using German Short Rows. Once you've

completed the number of short rows specified in the pattern, bring the double stitches together with a BRK. It really is that simple! (Photo 3)

WRAP & TURN SHORT ROWS

When working short rows in Stockinette Stitch, you will W&T (wrap and turn) to create your short rows, then pick up the wrapped stitches when you work over them after the short rows are complete.

W&T (knit)

Step 1: Keeping the yarn in back, slip the next stitch purlwise.

Step 2: Bring the yarn forward as if to purl.

Step 3: Slip the stitch from the RH needle back to the LH needle.

Step 4: Turn the work so the purl side is facing you, ready to purl.

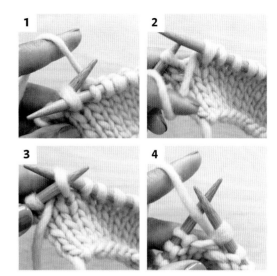

W&T (purl)

Step 1: Keeping the yarn in front, slip the next stitch purlwise.

Step 2: Bring the yarn back as if to knit.

Step 3: Slip the stitch from the RH needle back to the LH needle.

Step 4: Turn the work so the knit side is facing you, ready to knit.

continues

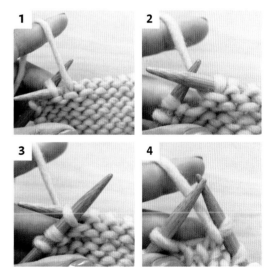

Picking up the wrapped stitch (knit)

Step 1: Pick up the wrap with the RH needle from front to back.

Step 2: Then insert the RH needle into the stitch that is wrapped. Knit the wrap and the stitch together.

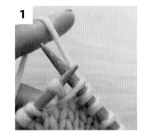
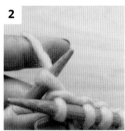

Picking up the wrapped stitch (purl)

Step 1: Pick up the wrap with the RH needle from back to front.

Step 2: Place the wrap onto the LH needle, over the stitch it's wrapping. Purl together the wrap and the stitch that is wrapped.

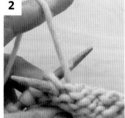

Picking up a purl wrap on the knit side when working in the round

Step 1: Work up to the wrapped stitch. Insert the needle from back to front under the wrap and into the stitch it's wrapping.

Step 2: Knit the wrap together with the wrap stitch, pulling the stitch that was wrapped to the right side of the fabric while the wrap falls to the wrong side.

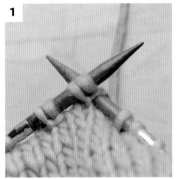

JOINING SHORT ROWS

Joining short rows allows us to join one section of knitting to another in the same row seamlessly. It's perfect for joining collars to the back of a neck and shaping shoulders. You'll work back and forth, making one section longer than the other, using a slip knit pass (skp) to join the elongated section to the section that will remain the same length throughout.

Joining on the knit side

Step 1: Work to the stitch specified in your pattern. (Photo 1)

Step 2: Slip 1 knitwise wyib, knit 1, pass the slipped stitch over. (Photo 2)

Step 3: Turn the work so the purl side is facing and you're ready to purl in the other direction. Slip 1 purlwise wyif, pulling the yarn taut, and work to end. (Photo 3)

Repeat Steps 1 to 3 to join stitches to the knit side of the work.

Joining on the purl side

Step 1: Work to the stitch specified in your pattern. Purl the next 2 stitches together. (Photo 4)

Step 2: Turn the work so the knit side is facing and you're ready to knit in the other direction. Slip 1 purlwise wyib, pulling the yarn taut, and work to end. (Photo 5)

Repeat Steps 1 and 2 to join stitches to the purl side of the work.

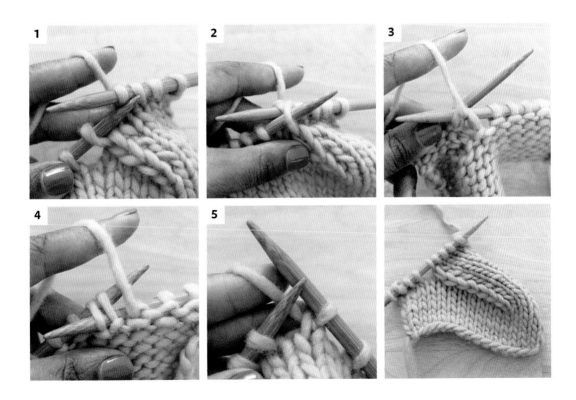

seamless knitting

You can create seamless garments by knitting in the round on circular and double pointed needles! When reading a chart, read every row from right to left. If you have only knit flat scarves and blankets, this section is especially for you!

KNITTING IN THE ROUND ON CIRCULAR NEEDLES

I own one single pair of straight needles and still remember that one time I used them. They are 20" [50 cm]-long size US 50 [25 mm]. I grasped them with fists crossed in front of me, a fedora on my head, my right big toe pressed against the shutter release of my camera remote. And I made a picture. I took one picture with the long, beautiful things. As a teenage knitter, buying circular needles was definitely more economical—one pair can be used for many different types of projects. Use a circular needle shorter in length than the circumference of the item you are knitting when working in the round; you want the stitches to fit comfortably around the circular and meet at the tips without stretching.

Here are some perks to working on circular needles:

- I can use the same circular needle to make flat rectangles or seamless tubes.

- I will lose just one needle, not one of a pair, and somehow that feels better.

- I knit on the train without jabbing my neighbors with my elbows.

- No seams to sew!

Step 1: Push the last and the first of the cast on stitches to the tips of the needles. Before working the first stitch to join the round, be sure your stitches are not twisted. The cast-on edge should run along the bottom of the needle all the way around without looping over the cable.

Step 2: Place a marker on the RH needle to mark the beginning of the round. With the working yarn, knit or purl the first stitch on the LH needle as specified in the pattern. Pull the working yarn taut so the first and last stitches come together snugly.

Step 3: Work around to the marker and slip the marker. Every time you reach the marker, you have completed one round.

1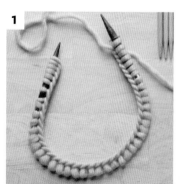

2

3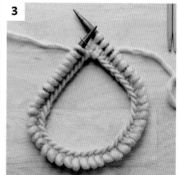

KNITTING IN THE ROUND ON DOUBLE POINTED NEEDLES

We use double pointed needles (dpns) to work in the round on small circumferences. This tutorial covers how to evenly divide stitches onto 3 dpns and how to work with a 4th needle.

Step 1: Cast on the number of stitches onto one of the dpns. (Photo 1)

Step 2: Slip a third of the stitches purlwise onto a 2nd dpn. Repeat with the 3rd dpn. It's okay if you have 1 or 2 more stitches on one dpn. (Photo 2)

Step 3: Arrange the needles to cross one over the other, so the working yarn is coming from the RH needle. Make sure the stitches are not twisted around any of the needles. The cast on edge should face downward on all three needles. (Photo 3)

Step 4: To mark the beginning of the round, place a marker on the RH needle between the first and last cast on stitch. Using the last needle with working yarn, knit or purl the first stitch on the first needle as specified in the pattern to secure the marker. (Photo 4)

Step 5: Using the 4th (empty) needle, work the rest of the stitches on the first dpn until all stitches are on the working needle. (Photo 5)

Repeat Step 5 to continue working in the round.

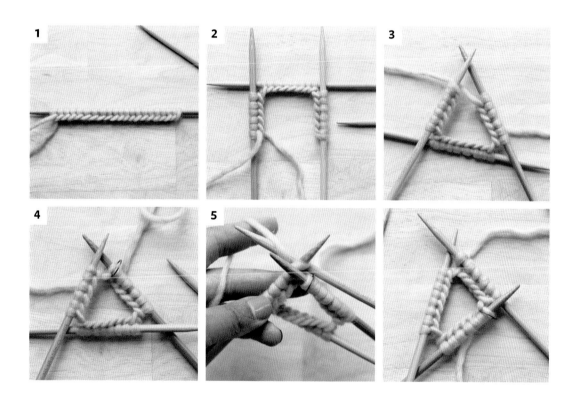

CROCHET SEAM

Crochet seams are magical. We will use a crochet hook to intentionally add an additional stitch to the fabric, picking up a horizonal ladder between 2 stitches from a designated area near the cast on edge. Crochet seams create added depth and structure in a piece by tightening the surrounding area, eliminating looseness. They will also lift the cast on edge where it is placed. I use this technique in several projects within this book. These seams make a significant difference in the overall look, fit, and construction of a piece.

Crochet seams are made with the WS facing; they appear as a single column of knit stitches on the WS of the fabric and a single column of purl stitches on the RS of the work. Crochet seams are strategically placed—where to pick up this additional stitch is specified in each pattern. When adding a crochet seam while the work is in progress, we pick up and knit a seam stitch, placing the seam stitch on the needle and decreasing the seam stitch away by knitting it together with its neighboring stitch. We'll also place the seam stitch on the needle without decreasing it to increase our stitch count. And sometimes we'll put the seam stitch on a removable stitch marker, returning to it later to continue the seam stitch along the same path. When adding crochet seams to a finished piece, we secure the seam stitch with the bind off tail before weaving in the end. Here are step-by-step instructions for how to make crochet seams.

Make a crochet seam
Step 1: Turn the work to the WS. Insert the crochet hook from top to bottom under the horizontal ladder between the 2 stitches specified in the pattern. (Photos 1 and 2)

Step 2: Twist the hook so the hook is right side up to twist the ladder and close the hole. (Photo 3)

Step 3: Insert the hook under the next ladder up. (Photo 4)

Step 4: Pull the ladder through the loop on the hook. (Photo 5)

Repeat Steps 3 and 4 until all the ladders in the column are picked up. (Photo 6)

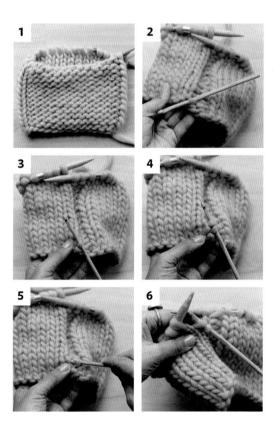

**Decrease a crochet seam stitch
while the work is in progress**

Step 1: With the WS still facing, place the seam stitch on the RH needle, being careful not to twist the stitch. (Photo 1)

Step 2: Turn to RS of work. (Photo 2)

Step 3: Decrease with either a k2tog—knitting the seam stitch together with the next stitch (Photo 3)—or skp, knitting the seam stitch and slipping the last stitch over (Photos 4 to 6). Which decrease to use is specified in the pattern.

Compare Photo 2 to Photo 6. Notice the difference between the tightness of the knit stitches and the lifting of the cast on edge.

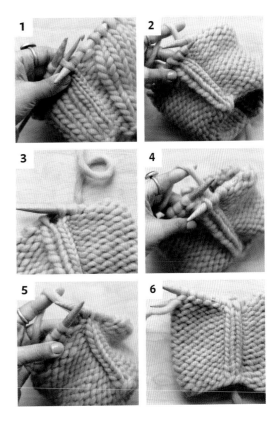

**Decrease a crochet seam stitch
when added to a finished piece**

Step 1: With the WS still facing and the last loop on the hook, thread a tapestry needle with the bind off tail closest to the seam stitch.

Step 2: Weave the tail through the seam stitch(es) to fasten off, weaving the tail in at least 2" [5 cm] deep to secure it to the WS.

finishing like a boss

I'm the kind of knitter who loves a good seam. It's the satisfying feeling of accomplishment to see the pieces come together that I like the most. These are the ones I use most often, and they really do create the kind of professional finish that makes you feel like a BOSS.

seaming

SEAMING BIND OFF TO BIND OFF

This technique creates a visible seam on both sides.

Step 1: To begin, cut a sewing tail 3 times the length of the seam and thread it onto a tapestry needle. When possible, use the working yarn attached to one of the pieces. Bring the bound-off edges together with the RS facing. Skip the first half of the first stitch, inserting the tapestry needle under the second half of the first stitch and half of the next, and pull the yarn through.

Step 2: Insert the tapestry needle into the corresponding V stitch on the other side, come back out through the next stitch, and pull the yarn through.

Step 3: Repeat Step 2, inserting the tapestry needle into the center of the stitches on each side, going under half of one stitch and back out half of another, working from right to left. Gently tighten the seam after joining each stitch to prevent breaking the sewing seam.

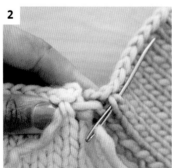

SEAMING BIND OFF TO SELVEDGE

You will work horizontally across the bind off edge and vertically up the selvedge edge to join these two edges together.

Step 1: Cut a sewing tail 3 times the length of the seam and thread it onto a tapestry needle. When possible, use the working yarn attached to one of the pieces. Bring bind off and selvedge edges together with the RS facing. (Photo 1)

Step 2: Insert the tapestry needle into the center of the first stitch along the bind off edge, skipping the first half of the first stitch, and pull the yarn through. (Photo 2)

Step 3: Insert the needle under the ladder created between the 2 outermost stitches along the selvedge. (Photo 3)

Repeat Steps 2 and 3, picking up a V stitch along the bind off for every ladder on the selvedge edge. (Photo 4)

Sometimes, the selvedge edge is longer and there are more places to pick up along that edge. To ease these two sides together such that the edges are flush and in alignment, pick up 2 rows on the selvedge edge for every 1 stitch along the bind off. (Photo 5)

Gently tighten the seam after joining each stitch to prevent breaking the sewing seam. The seam will fall to the WS of the work. (Photo 6)

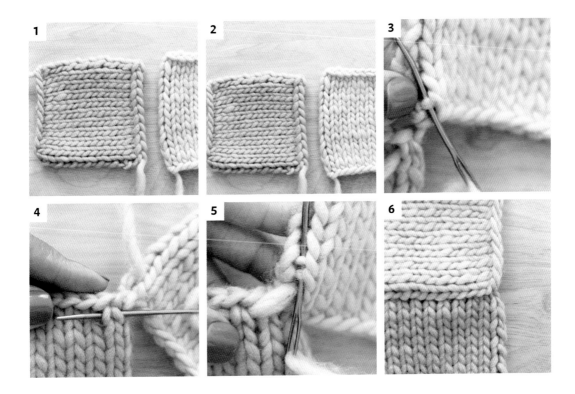

MATTRESS STITCH

Mattress stitch creates a nearly invisible seam on the RS of the work.

Each row of knitting makes a horizontal ladder between stitches, and you can see this ladder at the edge of the work. When we have 20 rows, we also have 20 ladders. To join selvedge edge to selvedge edge of Stockinette Stitch, we can join 2 ladder rows from one side to 2 ladder rows on the other, or 1 ladder row from one side to 1 ladder row on the other.

Step 1: Align the two pieces you want to seam with the RS facing you. When possible, use an existing tail already attached to the work to seam pieces together. Thread the tapestry needle with the tail and draw the needle from back to front through the edge on the other piece where you want to begin the seam. Here I'm using the tail left from the Long Tail Cast On. When you need a sewing tail, cut 3 times the length of the seam you wish to sew. (Photo 1)

Step 2: Take the tapestry needle back to the first piece and pick up the ladder just above the initial entry point or the cast on edge. Sometimes you'll have to tug on the outermost stitch to see the horizontal ladder. Be careful not to pick up yarn from the edge stitches themselves. (Photo 2)

Step 3: Take the needle back to the second piece and pick up the next bar above. Work vertically, alternating back and forth, to pick up the next horizontal bar

above the last place you entered. It's best and faster to draw through an inch or two [2.5 to 5 cm] loosely before gently pulling the yarn to cinch the pieces together and close the seam. Don't pull too tightly, or the fabric can buckle. When one side is longer than the other and you're trying to ease two pieces together, pick up 2 ladders on the longer side for every one ladder on the shorter side. (Photo 3)

Step 4: Whenever possible, use the tail attached to the last bind off stitch to bring the bind off edges on each side together. Insert the tapestry needle under the first bind off stitch opposite the piece attached to the tail, then back into the center of the stitch on the other side.

KITCHENER STITCH

Kitchener Stitch joins live stitches together with an invisible seam.

To begin, cut a sewing tail 3 times the length you wish to sew and thread it onto a tapestry needle. Whenever possible, use the working yarn attached to one of the pieces. Hold the needles with the live stitches parallel, WS facing each other, in your left hand.

Step 1: Insert the tapestry needle through the first stitch on the back needle knit-wise. Leave the stitch on the back needle. (Photo 1)

Step 2: Insert the tapestry needle through the first stitch on the front needle purlwise and pull the yarn through, leaving the stitch on the front needle. (Photo 2)

Step 3: Insert the tapestry needle through the first stitch on the back needle purlwise and pull the yarn through, dropping the stitch from the back needle. (Photo 3)

Step 4: Insert the tapestry needle through the first stitch on the back needle knitwise and pull the yarn through, leaving the stitch on the back needle. (Photo 4)

Step 5: Insert the tapestry needle through the first stitch on the front needle knitwise and pull the yarn through, dropping the stitch on the front needle. (Photo 5)

Step 6: Insert the tapestry needle through the first stitch on the front needle purlwise and pull the yarn through, leaving the stitch on the front needle. (Photo 6)

Repeat Step 3 to Step 6 until all the stitches have been worked. You'll insert your tapestry needle into each of the last stitches twice, as established, before dropping the stitches off the needles.

Remember, you are making an extra row of knitting rather than sewing together a seam—pay careful attention to your tension so it looks like the rows above and below. Adjust the tension of the sewing tail as you go along, being sure not to pull too tightly. (Photo 7)

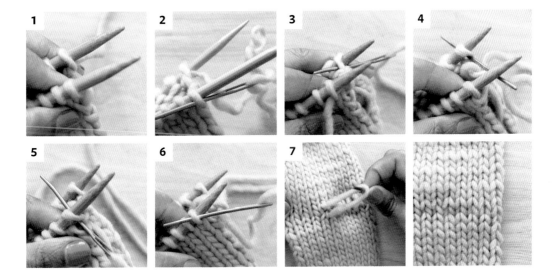

washing and blocking

When we submerge a knit in water, it undergoes a profound change in just seconds. The fabric becomes lighter, stitches more at ease, seams flatter. I wash and block all of my knits unless the yarn label recommends dry cleaning.

Step 1: Fill the washing basin with cool water and add a gentle woolen wash. I especially love Purl Soho's Sweater Soap. It is made in the USA from organic plant-based saponified oils. It's rinse-free and especially good for hand knits.

Step 2: Once you've sewn all the seams and weaved in all your ends, let the finished garment soak for 10 to 15 minutes. Do not agitate.

Step 3: If you're using a soap that requires a rinse, go ahead and gently rinse until you no longer see soapsuds. If rinsing is not necessary, pull your knit out and squeeze out the excess water. Do not wring.

Step 4: Reshape the garment on a clean surface to your finished measurements and let it dry completely. I use a small, inexpensive fan to speed up the drying time.

Step 5: Steam blocking with an iron is my favorite part of the finishing process. This is where we can flatten seams or help edges lie a little flatter when needed. Place a blocking cloth or white paper towel over your piece so the wool does not come in direct contact with the hot iron. Gently move the iron over the cloth, letting the steam relax the fabric. Add a little pressure to the areas that need a bit of flattening.

Step 6. Let the item dry completely again, and then try that baby on!

simple stitches

Each pattern uses one of these six modern fabrics, all beginner friendly, relatively simple, and easy to memorize.* I made all my swatches using a chunkyweight yarn, getting 12 to 14 stitches to 4" [10 cm] on a US 10 [6 mm]. With basic fabrics, there will be more space to practice and master modern edges, construction, and finishing skills. I share my favorite aspects of these stitches and basic row instructions to make your beloved gauge swatch. You may already be familiar with one or all of these stitches, so feel free to go ahead and dive right into your favorite patterns! Make these swatches with the small bundles in your stash to practice techniques and seaming along the edges. Put them on a key ring for later reference as you make other patterns in this book and venture off to design simple-stitch knits of your own. I include my favorite way of trimming or not trimming each stitch.

* The Terran Hat uses the highly textured and not-so-simple Bloom Stitch, also known as the Daisy Stitch. It definitely falls outside of my Modern Guide to Knitting framework. It's so cool, though, I couldn't resist adding it to the book!

garter stitch

A reversible fabric, the same on both sides. We work Garter by knitting back and forth in rows, and alternating one purl round and one knit round when working in the round. Each Garter ridge is made up of 2 rows or 2 rounds. When working flat, slip the first stitch of every row knitwise and pull taut. This gives your edge a nice, neat finish.

SWATCH GARTER WITH A SLIP STITCH SELVEDGE
Using the Long Tail Cast On, CO 20 or any number of stitches.

Row 1: slip 1 knitwise, knit to end.

stockinette stitch

Stockinette is timeless. Knit stitches on one side, purl stitches on the other. Knit all rows when working in the round; purl one row then knit one row when working flat. The edges curl toward the purl side of the fabric.

SWATCH STOCKINETTE WITH NO SELVEDGES OR BORDERS
Using the Long Tail Cast On, CO 20 or any number of stitches.

Row 1 (RS): knit.

Row 2: purl.

Repeat Rows 1 and 2 for 4" [10 cm] or desired length, ending with a WS row. Using the Basic Knit Bind Off, BO all stitches knitwise.

reverse stockinette

The other side of Stockinette Stitch. A twofer.

SWATCH REVERSE STOCKINETTE WITH NO SELVEDGES OR BORDERS
Using the Long Tail Cast On, CO 20 or any number of stitches.

Row 1 (RS): purl.

Row 2: knit.

Repeat Rows 1 and 2 for 4" [10 cm] or desired length, ending with a RS row. Using the Basic Knit Bind Off, BO all stitches purlwise.

1×1 rib

A 1×1 Rib fabric is the same on both sides—reversible and stretchy.

SWATCH 1×1 RIB WITH A SLIP STITCH SELVEDGE
Using the Long Tail Tubular Cast On, CO 21 or an odd number of stitches.

Row 1 (RS): k1, [k1, p1] to last stitch, slip 1 purlwise wyif.

Row 2: k1tbl, [p1, k1] to last stitch, slip 1 purlwise wyif.

Repeat Rows 1 and 2 for 4" [10 cm] or desired length, ending with a WS row. Using the Tubular Bind Off or the Basic Knit Bind Off, BO all stitches, knitting the knits and purling the purls.

brioche stitch

Here's what you need to know about Brioche: it's tricky and fun.* When counting stitches, count only the purl and knit columns—the yarn overs are not included in the stitch count; the knit and yarn over pair counts as a single stitch. When you count rows on the RS, each stitch in a knit column is really 2 rows worked. Brioche stitch is reversible, so place a removable marker to mark the RS of the work, or you may forget which side is which. In this book, you'll explore several Brioche techniques, including the basic stitch pattern, increasing in Brioche, and working short rows in Brioche.

SWATCH BRIOCHE WITH A 2-STITCH GARTER BORDER AND SLIP STITCH SELVEDGE

Using the Long Tail Tubular Cast On, CO 21 or an odd number of stitches.

Foundation Row (WS): slip 1 knitwise wyib, k1, [k1, sl1yo] to last 3 stitches, k3.

Row 1 (RS): slip 1 knitwise wyib, k1, [sl1yo, BRK] to last 3 stitches, sl1yo, k2.

Row 2: slip 1 knitwise wyib, k1, [BRK, sl1yo] to last 3 stitches, BRK, k2.

Repeat Rows 1 and 2 for 4" [10 cm] or desired length, ending with Row 1.

Last Row: slip 1 knitwise wyib, k1, [BRK, p1] to last 3 stitches, BRK, k2.

BO all stitches using Tubular Bind Off or the Basic Knit Bind Off, knitting the knits and 2-stitch Garter border and purling the purls.

---

* Shout-out to Nancy Marchant, also known as the "Mother of Brioche," who coined the Brioche terms and abbreviations used in this book. She creates beautiful flower motifs and two-color Brioche patterns, if you'd like to explore this stitch pattern more.

SL1YO

Slip 1 with yarn over. Slipping 1 stitch with a yarn over counts as 1 stitch. When working flat in rows, you'll work a BRK on the following row. When working in the round, you'll work a BRP on the following round. You'll work the sl1yo the same way when working flat and in the round.

Step 1: Bring the working yarn under the RH needle to the front of the work.

Step 2: Slip the next stitch purlwise, then bring the working yarn over the RH needle to the back of the work. (Photo 1)

BRK

Brioche knit.

Knit the next stitch together with its corresponding yarn over from the previous row. (Photo 2)

BRP

Brioche purl.

Purl the next stitch together with its corresponding yarn over from the previous row. (Photo 3)

BRKYOBRK

Brioche knit, yarn over, brioche knit, a 2-stitch increase worked in brioche fabric.

Step 1: BRK, leaving the stitch on the LH needle, yarn over, then BRK into the same stitch. (Photo 4)

Step 2: On the following row, work the BRKYOBRK as sl1yo, k1, sl1yo.

cables

This is where we get to knit stitches out of order on purpose. Once you learn the simple act of twisting stitches over one another with a third needle, you'll be able to dive into most cable patterns with excitement. They do take more time to create. This tutorial shows two cables worked side by side and leaning in opposite directions.

SWATCH CABLE WITH A 4-STITCH REVERSE STOCKINETTE BORDER
Using the Long Tail Cast On, CO 20 stitches (12 stitches for Cable + 8 for Reverse Stockinette Stitch border)

Foundation Row (WS): k4, p12, k4.

Row 1 (RS): p4, C6B, C6F, p4.

Row 2: k4, p12, k4.

Row 3: p4, k12, p4.

Row 4: k4, p12, k4.

Repeat Rows 1 to 4 for 4" [10 cm] or desired length, ending with Row 4. Using the Basic Knit Bind Off, BO all stitches, knitting the knits and purling the purls.

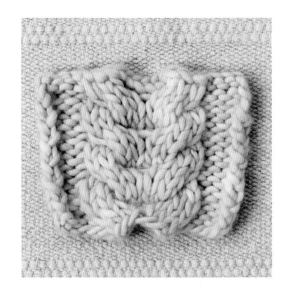

C6B

Cable 6 back. A right-leaning cable.

Step 1: Work to the 6 stitches you will be cabling. Slip 3 stitches purlwise from the LH needle to a CN or DPN. (Photo 1)

Step 2: To make the cable slant to the right, place the CN at the back of your work and behind the working yarn. (Photo 2)

Step 3: *Skip* the 3 stitches held on the CN and knit 3 stitches from the LH needle. (Photo 3)

Step 4: Knit the 3 stitches off of the CN. (Photo 4)

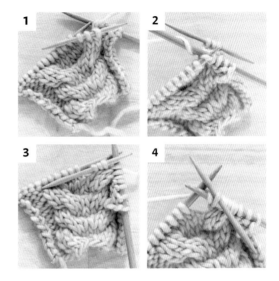

C6F

Cable 6 front. A left-leaning cable.

Step 1: Work to the 6 stitches you will be cabling. Slip 3 stitches purlwise from the LH needle to a CN or DPN.

Step 2: To make the cable slant to the left, place the CN to the front of your work and in front of the working yarn. (Photo 1)

Step 3: *Skip* the 3 stitches held on the CN and knit 3 stitches from the LH needle. (Photo 2)

Step 4: Knit the 3 stitches off of the CN. (Photo 3)

PART III

patterns

These patterns are named for words that express the human need to make by hand, for solitude, time in nature, a sense of belonging, community, and love. Imagine every word is a brightly lit room, designed for our comfort as we explore who we are, what we want, and how we are getting there. Each essay can be read independent of the others, and all are interconnected. You will be visited by a cohort of revolutionaries who encourage us to own our power. Each design transports us to another dimension—to a rich and sometimes difficult past, to a mindful present, and to our hopeful future.

May you find answers to the questions you have not yet known to ask. May you make for making's sake and know all good things are possible. Every stitch you knit can be a self-care practice. Knitting is our constant companion as we grow and expand our capacity for joy.

tombolo

tuhm·bow·low

---

noun

a bar of sand or gathering of small, rounded pebbles
joining an island to the mainland

A tombolo is a sandy isthmus, a narrow strip of land with sea on either side, forming a link between two larger areas of land. It can also be translated to *pillow* or *cushion*. When attached by a tombolo, the smaller area is known as a tied island. Imagine if every day, every moment, we are tethered to our limitless imaginations. Our project bags stuffed with yarn, recipes, sewing patterns, watercolors, the songs we sing, and the pages of our notebooks are a short walking distance way. If the daily and necessary tasks of being human are the mainland, our creativity is the tied island. The tombolo is every action we intentionally take to connect the two. The phrases we use around our hobbies often position them as secondary, distant, and unconnected to what we are "supposed" to be doing.

We must unlearn the othering language disconnecting us from the things that fill us with delight.

Your passion projects are not a side gig. They are a passport.

Your dreams are not on the back burner, they are shimmering and piping hot.

It's not a hustle, it's a journey.

We also must deal with memories of the disapproving parent or teacher, society's limiting definitions of success, and the people who will trample our work.

I landed my first managerial job with company benefits at age thirty. I had been running my online shop for four years. I was determined to get my finances in order and start saving money. The job was a tombolo within itself, allowing me to comfortably traverse homeownership goals and the trial-and-error process of developing my own creative business plan. Tasked first with renovating our service desk, I went to work making surveys, talking to coworkers, and finding some way to standardize the information board. In another part of the building, we updated a chalkboard to share special announcements. This would work so well for the service desk, too! I ran out and purchased a chalkboard with a sticky back. I used my own money because if it didn't work out, at least it wouldn't cost the company. I rearranged a few things on the wall to give the chalkboard a try. In an instant, the wall became café chic. I planned to use chalk paint to draw an espresso-menu-inspired template for all relevant service desk information. The service desk workers, who often passed their time playing sudoku and writing term papers, could update as needed. But the next day, I learned my supervisor had taken the chalkboard off the wall and thrown it in the garbage. I was reimbursed $32 and change. The experience was a pivotal moment in my life. Demoralizing and traumatic. Never had anything like that ever happened to me. My mother let nine-year-old me create massive crayon murals on my bedroom walls. I was the only person in my junior high school to be accepted into LaGuardia High School, a specialized school for performing and visual arts. And even though I've spent a great deal of my life deeply insecure, I knew my gifts were inherent and natural. I have purpose, placed on this earth for a reason. I have the capacity to create good work. If ever I forget, someone always seems to be around to remind me. This was the first time someone had made my work literal trash with no questions asked.

My time at that job was a constant battle against apathy and jadedness. I left after three years to pursue my design work full-time. I don't think many of us realize how closely linked creative deficiency is to our unhappiness. Creativity is an ever-present buzzing of possibility, and it flows through everything feeding our purpose. Creativity gives us access to what we are and have always been. There will be people, societal systems, and technology that will attempt to lock the doors and construct the barriers to that possibility. They don't want us to try. We keep going, placing stepping stones along the path as a guide for someone else. Every action you take, however small, in service of your vision, is like picking the lock and finding a window. "This means," says Nina Simone, "using everything you've got inside you sometimes to barely make a note, or even if you strain to sing—you sing. So sometimes I sound like gravel and sometimes I sound like coffee and cream." In nature, a tombolo takes many years of letting go, letting in, a gathering of small particles over many years.

Is it possible to carve out twenty minutes to gather the materials needed for your tombolo? What can improve access to your creative island retreat? It is never too late, we are never too old, there *is* enough time.

tombolo cowl

collar

Work Crochet Chain Provisional Cast On as follows: Using US I-9 [5.5 mm] crochet hook, chain 44 stitches and fasten off. Using 16" [40.5 cm] circular needles size US 11 [8 mm], pick up and knit 42 stitches into the back loops of the crochet chain.

Joining Round: pm, k1 to join in the round, k20, pm of contrasting color, k21.

Increase Round: p1, k1, p1, [kfb] 16 times, k1, p1, slm, k21— 16 stitches increased; 58 stitches total.

Round 1: p1, [k1, p1] 18 times, slm, p2, k17, p2.

Note: Continue to slip markers.

Repeat Round 1 for 30 more rounds or until piece measures approximately 9" [23 cm] from cast on edge.

shape neck

Decrease Round: p1, skpp, work 1×1 Rib to 4 stitches before next marker, sk2p, p1, slm, p2, knit to last 2 stitches, p2— 4 stitches decreased; 54 stitches total.

Working as established, repeat Decrease Round every 6th round 3 more times—42 stitches.

crochet seams

Turn Collar inside out so WS is facing. Beginning above cast on edge, being careful not to pick up provisional cast on and using size F-5 [3.5 mm] crochet hook, make a total of 4 crochet seams (see page 58), one on each side of the 1×1 Rib next to the purl stitch, and one on each side of the 17 Reverse Stockinette stitches. Work the crochet seams until all ladder rows are picked up to the last round. Slip

MATERIALS

3 skeins Ocean by the Sea "Thicc" (100% merino wool; 76 yards [70 m]/100 grams) in Sage Blush, or approximately 228 yards [210 m] of chunky-weight yarn

16" [40.5 cm] circular needles size US 10½ [6.5 mm] and US 11 [8 mm]

Crochet hooks size US F-5 [3.75 mm] and US I-9 [5.5 mm]

Removable stitch markers

Tapestry needle

Scissors

GAUGE

10 stitches and 18 rows = 4" [10 cm] over Stockinette Stitch using US 11 [8 mm] needles or size needed to obtain gauge

FINISHED MEASUREMENTS

Circumference of collar at largest point, slightly stretched: Approx. 24" [60 cm]

Circumference along bind off edge at shoulder: Approx. 34" [86.5 cm]

Length along center front: Approx. 10" [25.5 cm]

each seam stitch onto a removable stitch marker to secure. Once the Collar is joined and the shoulder is complete, the crochet seams will continue along the cowl to the bind off edge.

join collar

With Collar still inside out, remove the scrap yarn from the provisional cast on edge and place 42 live stitches onto US 10½ [6.5 mm] circular needles. Weave in all ends before joining. Fold Collar in half so WS are facing and needles are parallel, with US 11 [8 mm] needle in front and US 10½ [6.5 mm] needle behind. PM on front needle to mark beginning of round.

Note: *Be sure to keep all removable stitch markers with live crochet seam stitches on hold to the RS of the work in front, so they do not get hidden between the two halves of the Collar after joining. You want to be able to keep the crochet seams going along the same line after bringing the Collar together. We'll reposition the markers to the WS after the joining.*

Using 16" [40.5 cm] circular needles size US 11 [8 mm] and working yarn, [p1 on front needle, insert needle into next knit stitch on front needle then into next 2 stitches on back needle and knit 3 stitches together] 10 times, p3, *[insert needle into next stitch on front needle then into next stitch on back needle and knit 2 stitches together] 2 times, [insert needle into next stitch on front needle then into next 2 stitches on back needle and knit 3 stitches together]; repeat from * 4 more times, [insert needle into next stitch on front needle then into next stitch on back needle and knit 2 stitches together] 2 times, p2—42 stitches.

Note: Carefully push seam stitches on removable stitch markers to the WS.

shape shoulder

Next Row (RS): remove marker, p1, pm of CC to mark new beginning of round, [k1, p1] 9 times, k1, pm, p3, pm, k17, pm, p3—42 stitches.

Increase Round 1: [k1, yo, k1] into next stitch, purl the purls and knit the knits to 1 stitch before next marker, [k1, yo, k1] into next stitch, slm, yo, purl to marker, yo, slm, k17, slm, yo, purl to end of round, yo—8 stitches increased; 50 stitches total.

Round 2: [k1, p1] to 3 stitches before next marker, k1, p1, k1, slm, *p1tbl, purl to 1 stitch before next marker, p1tbl,* slm, k17, slm, repeat from * to * once.

Increase Round 3: knit the knits and purl the purls to next marker, slm, yo, purl to next marker, yo, slm, k17, slm, yo, purl end of round, yo—4 stitches increased; 54 stitches total.

Round 4: knit the knits and purl the purls to next marker, slm, *p1tbl, purl to 1 stitch before next marker, p1tbl,* slm, k17, slm, repeat from * to * once.

Repeat Increase Round 1 to Round 4 twice more, then repeat Increase Round 1 and Row 2 once more—86 stitches.

continue crochet seams

Reposition the seam stitches on the WS of the work, carefully moving the stitch over if necessary, to continue each crochet seam along the same column of stitches.

Next Round: *turn to WS, remove stitch marker from seam stitch. Using US F-5 [3.5 mm] crochet hook, continue crochet seam along work to needles, placing the seam stitch on the RH needle after working the last ladder. Turn to RS, purl 1 seam stitch,* [k1, p1] to 1 stitch before next marker, k1, remove marker from needle, repeat from * to *, purl to next marker, remove marker from needle, repeat from * to *, k17, remove marker, repeat from * to *, p18, removing marker—90 stitches.

Next Round: [k1, p1] 17 times, k1, using US I-9 [5.5 mm] crochet hook and 3 strands of yarn held together, BO 55 stitches using Crochet Bind Off. Cut 3 feet [3 m] of tail from one strand of yarn and 8" [20 cm] tails for the other 2 strands. Pull the last loop remaining after the bind off up and out to fasten off. With RS facing and using tapestry needle and longer tail, BO remaining 35 stitches using the Tubular Bind Off.

finishing

Weave in all ends. Soak the cowl in cool water using a gentle woolen soap for 10 to 15 minutes. Reshape and lay flat to dry.

allay

uh·lei

---

verb

to make quiet, calm; alleviate or lighten in intensity;
put to rest

"IT'S IMPORTANT TO KNOW WHO THE REAL ENEMY IS AND TO KNOW THE VERY SERIOUS FUNCTION OF RACISM, WHICH IS DISTRACTION. IT KEEPS YOU FROM DOING YOUR WORK. IT KEEPS YOU EXPLAINING OVER AND OVER YOUR REASON FOR BEING. IT MAY VERY WELL BE LEFT TO ARTISTS TO GRAPPLE WITH THIS FACT.

FOR ART FOCUSES ON THE SINGLE GRAIN OF RICE, THE TREE-SHAPED SCAR AND THE NAMES OF PEOPLE SHIPPED NOT ONLY THE NUMBER. AND TO THE ARTIST ONE CAN ONLY SAY: NOT TO BE CONFUSED. YOU DON'T WASTE YOUR ENERGY FIGHTING THE FEVER. YOU MUST ONLY FIGHT THE DISEASE. AND THE DISEASE IS NOT RACISM. IT IS GREED AND THE STRUGGLE FOR POWER.

AND I URGE YOU TO BE CAREFUL FOR THERE IS A DEADLY PRISON. A PRISON THAT IS ERECTED WHEN ONE SPENDS ONE'S LIFE FIGHTING PHANTOMS, CONCENTRATING ON MYTHS, AND EXPLAINING OVER AND OVER TO THE CONQUEROR YOUR LANGUAGE, YOUR LIFESTYLE, YOUR HISTORY, YOUR HABITS. AND YOU DON'T HAVE TO DO IT ANYMORE. YOU CAN GO AHEAD AND TALK STRAIGHT TO ME."

—Toni Morrison

To read Morrison's work gives me the tools to chisel, to build my own table and fashion my own crown. I can see myself in the tangle of her locs, my dark skin reflected through the pride in her eyes. I get to be a happy Black person vibing with my plants and dancing to my playlists. She shares with me the richness of my history, heartbreakingly resilient and mine. She gives me access to who I am and keeps me at attention.

When I think of Toni, I am allayed. Fear leaves my body, and my potential is limitless.

She is the machete cutting away the tangled mess leveled against us for centuries. She does not doubt me. She holds me in high esteem. When I think about the stories I want to tell, the people I hope to reach, I ready myself for tea with Toni. With her, there is no debating the color of the sky.

Write her a poem.

Tell her your story.

Morrison says, "You want to fly, you got to give up the shit that weighs you down." The Allay Jacket is cropped with a lifted back, and the front leans forward.

allay jacket

collar

BEGIN LEFT SIDE OF COLLAR

Work I-Cord Cast On as follows: using Crochet Chain Provisional Cast On, crochet hook, and scrap yarn, chain 5 stitches and fasten off. Using dpns, pick up and knit 3 stitches into the back loops of the crochet chain. Work I-Cord for 15 rows. Slip 3 stitches onto 16" [40.5 cm] circular needles, and pick up and knit 13 stitches into the top half of the first stitch of each row along the I-Cord. Carefully remove the scrap yarn from the provisional cast on. Slip the 3 live stitches onto the RH needle with the purl side facing you and working yarn in front—19 stitches.

Foundation Row 1 (WS): k5, sl1yo, k7, sl1yo, k2, slip 3 purlwise wyif.

Foundation Row 2 (RS): k5, BRK, sl1yo, k4, pm, k1, sl1yo, BRK, k2, slip 3 purlwise wyif.

Increase Row (WS): k5, sl1yo, BRK, k1, slm, yo, knit to last 7 stitches, BRK, sl1yo, k2, slip 3 purlwise wyif—1 stitch increased; 20 stitches total.

Next Row (RS): k5, BRK, sl1yo, knit to 1 stitch before marker, k1tbl, slm, k1, sl1yo, BRK, k2, slip 3 purlwise wyif.

Repeat last 2 rows 34 more times—54 stitches.

Note: After working a few rows, place removable marker to mark the wrong side of work.

SHAPE LEFT SIDE OF COLLAR

Garter Short Row 1 (WS): k5, sl1yo, BRK, k1, remove marker, knit to last 8 stiches, T&S, slip 1 knitwise wyib, knit to last 7 stitches, sl1yo, BRK, k2, slip 3 purlwise wyif.

Garter Short Row 2 (WS): k5, sl1yo, BRK, knit to 2 stitches before last turn (you will be 2 stitches before the short row gap), T&S, knit to last 7 stitches, sl1yo, BRK, k2, slip 3 purlwise wyif.

MATERIALS

14 (17, 18, 20, 23, 18, 26, 32) skeins of Ocean by the Sea "Thicc" in Terracotta (100% merino wool; 76 yards/100 grams) or approximately 1,065 (1,225, 1,344, 1,480, 1,715, 1,935, 2,145, 2,405) yards [975 (1,120, 1,235, 1,350, 1,565, 1,770, 1,960, 2,200) m] of chunky-weight yarn

16" [40.5 cm] circular needles size US 10½ [6.5 mm]

24" [60 cm] circular needles size US 10½ [6.5 mm]

40" circular needles size US 10½ [6.5 mm]

Double pointed needles size US 10½ [6.5 mm]

Crochet hook size US K-10½ [6.5 mm]

Stitch markers

Scrap yarn

Tapestry needle

Scissors

FINISHED MEASUREMENTS

This piece is designed for a relaxed fit with 4–7" [10–18 cm] of ease. If you are between chest measurements, size down. Sample shown in size 45" [114 cm].

Chest circumference: 37 (41, 45, 48, 52, 57, 61, 65)" [94 (104, 114, 124.5, 134.5, 144.5, 155, 165) cm]

Waist to underarm (cropped side waist length): 8" [20 cm]

Circumference at upper arm: 12 (14, 16, 17½, 19½, 19½, 19½, 19½)" [30.5 (35.5, 40.5, 44.5, 49.5, 49.5, 49.5, 49.5) cm]

Sleeve length from underarm: 12½ (12½, 12½, 12½, 13½, 13½, 13½, 13½)" [31.5 (31.5, 31.5, 31.5, 34.5, 34.5, 34.5, 34.5) cm]

GAUGE

12 stitches and 22 rows = 4" [10 cm] over Garter Stitch using US 10½ [6.5 mm] needles or needle needed to obtain gauge

Repeat Short Row 2 for 15 more times.

Last Garter Short Row (WS): k5, sl1yo, BRK, k4, T&S, k4, sl1yo, BRK, k2, slip 3 purlwise.

Pick Up Garter Short Rows (WS): k5, sl1yo, BRK, k4, [KPK] 18 times, BRK, sl1yo, k2, slip 3 purlwise wyif.

Next Row (RS): k5, BRK, sl1yo, knit to last 7 stitches, sl1yo, BRK, k2, slip 3 purlwise wyif.

Next Row: k5, p1, BRK, knit to last 7 stitches, BRK, p1, k2, slip last 3 stitches to a dpn, turn the needle so the knit side is facing you, knit last 3 stiches onto the RH needle.

Slip stitches purlwise onto 24" [60 cm] circular needles and set aside.

BEGIN RIGHT SIDE OF COLLAR
Work I-Cord Cast On as for Left Side of Collar, repeating from * to *—19 stitches.

Foundation Row 1 (WS): k5, sl1yo, k7, sl1yo, k2, slip 3 purlwise wyif.

Foundation Row 2 (RS): k5, BRK, sl1yo, k1, pm, k4, sl1yo, BRK, k2, slip 3 purlwise wyif.

Increase Row (WS): k5, sl1yo, BRK, knit to marker, yo, slm, k1, BRK, sl1yo, k2, slip 3 purlwise wyif—1 stitch increased; 20 stitches total.

Next Row (RS): k5, BRK, sl1yo, k1, slm, k1tbl, knit to last 7 stitches, sl1yo, BRK, k2, slip 3 purlwise wyif.

Repeat last 2 rows 34 more times—54 stitches.

Next Row: k5, sl1yo, BRK, knit to marker, remove marker, k1, BRK, sl1yo, k2, slip 3 purlwise wyif.

SHAPE RIGHT SIDE OF COLLAR
Garter Short Row 1 (RS): k5, BRK, sl1yo, knit to last 8 stiches, T&S, knit to last 7 stitches, BRK, sl1yo, k2, slip 3 purlwise wyif.

Garter Short Row 2 (RS): k5, BRK, sl1yo, knit to 2 stitches before last turn, T&S, knit to last 7 stitches, BRK, sl1yo, k2, slip 3 purlwise wyif.

Repeat Garter Short Row 2 for 15 more times.

Last Short Row (RS): k5, BRK, sl1yo, k5, T&S, k4, BRK, sl1yo, k2, slip 3 purlwise wyif.

Pick Up Garter Short Rows (RS): k5, BRK, sl1yo, k4, [KPK] 18 times, sl1yo, BRK, k2, slip 3 purlwise wyif. Turn. With WS facing, slip the last 3 stitches purlwise onto a dpn, turn needle so the knit side is facing you, slip same 3 stitches back to LH needle.

Next Row (WS): k5, sl1yo, BRK, knit to last 7 stitches, BRK, sl1yo, k2, p3. Cut 100" [250 cm] of tail to sew the seam.

JOIN SIDES OF COLLAR
With WS facing each other and the Right Side of Collar and sewing yarn in front, join two sides together using Kitchener Stitch.

yoke

Lay Collar flat with the RS facing, the top edge of Collar at the bottom, and the cast on edges at the top. Using 40" [60 cm] circular, pick up and knit 110 stitches into every available stitch along lower edge of Collar as follows: With the RS facing and beginning at Left Front cast on edge, pick up and knit 107 stitches, picking up into the top half of the first stitch along the I-Cord Selvedge, leaving 2 stitches from the I-Cord visible on the RS; then with yarn in front, pick up 3 stitches as if to purl from the I-Cord and place on RH needle without knitting them to set up the I-Cord Selvedge.

Next Row (WS): k15, *pm, k2, sl1yo, k1, pm, k17, pm, k1, sl1yo, k2, pm*, k30; repeat from * to * one more time, k12, slip 3 purlwise wyif.

RAGLAN SHAPING

Increase Row (RS): *knit to next marker, yo, slm, k1, sl1yo, BRK, k1, slm, yo, knit to next marker, yo, slm, k1, BRK, sl1yo, k1, slm, yo,*; repeat from * to * one more time, knit to last 3 stitches, slip 3 purlwise wyif—8 stitches increased; 118 stitches total.

Next Row: *knit to 1 stitch before next marker, k1tbl, slm, k1, BRK, sl1yo, k1, slm, k1tbl, knit to 1 stitch before next marker, k1tbl, slm, k1, sl1yo, BRK, k1, slm, k1tbl*; repeat from * to * one more time, knit to last 3 stitches, slip 3 purlwise wyif.

Repeat last 2 rows 9 (12, 15, 17, 20, 20, 20) more times—190 (214, 238, 254, 278, 278, 278) stitches.

Work 10 (4, 0, 0, 0, 0, 0) rows even.

For sizes - (-, -, -, -, 57, 61, 65)"[- (-, -, -, -, 144.5, 155, 165) cm] only
Body Only Increase Row (RS): *knit to next marker, yo, slm, k1, sl1yo, BRK, k1, slm, knit to next marker, slm, k1, BRK, sl1yo, k1, slm, yo,*; repeat from * to * one more time, knit to last 3 stitches, slip 3 purlwise wyif—4 stitches increased.

Next Row: *knit to 1 stitch before next marker, k1tbl, slm, k1, BRK, sl1yo, k1, slm, knit to next marker, slm, k1, sl1yo, BRK, k1, slm, k1tbl*; repeat from * to * one more time, knit to last 3 stitches, slip 3 purlwise wyif.

Repeat last 2 rows 3 (6, 9) more times—294 (306, 318) stitches.

For all sizes
separate sleeves from body

Next Row (RS): k25 (28, 31, 33, 36, 40, 43, 46), slm, k1, sl1yo, BRK, k1, slm, k6 for Left Front, *slip next 36 (42, 48, 52, 58, 58, 58, 58) stitches purlwise onto scrap yarn for Sleeve, removing markers, and hold in front*, with working yarn, k48 (54, 60, 64, 70, 78, 84, 90) from Body for Back; repeat from * to * for second Sleeve, with working yarn, k6, slm, k1, BRK, sl1yo, k1, slm, knit to last 3 stitches, slip 3 purlwise wyif from body for Right Front.

body

Next Row (WS): knit to marker, slm, k1, BRK, sl1yo, k1, slm, knit to next marker, slm, k1, sl1yo, BRK, k1, slm, knit to last 3 stitches, slip 3 purlwise wyif—118 (130, 142, 150, 162, 178, 190, 202) stitches.

Next Row (RS): knit to marker, slm, k1, sl1yo, BRK, k1, slm, knit to next marker, slm, k1, BRK, sl1yo, k1, slm, knit to last 3 stitches, slip 3 purlwise wyif.

Repeat last 2 rows until piece measures 7½" [19 cm] from underarm, ending with a WS row.

Next Row (RS): knit to marker, remove marker, k1, p1, BRK, k1, remove marker, knit to next marker, remove marker, k1, BRK, p1, k1, remove marker, knit to last 3 stitches, slip 3 purlwise wyif.

I-CORD BIND OFF

Work I-Cord Bind Off as follows: *k2, skp, with yarn in back, slip 3 stitches from the RH needle back to LH needle; repeat from * until all stitches are worked and a total of 6 stitches remain. Using Kitchener Stitch, seam the I-Cord stitches together.

sleeves

RIGHT SLEEVE

Slip 36 (42, 48, 52, 58, 58, 58, 58) stitches purlwise to 16" [40.5 cm] circular needles. Join a new ball of yarn with RS facing, k2, sl1yo, BRK, knit to end, pick up and knit 3 stitches along underarm gusset to close gap, p1, pm for beginning of round—39 (45, 51, 55, 61, 61, 61, 61) stitches.

Decrease Gusset Round 1: p1, BRP, sl1yo, purl to last 2 stitches, p2tog—1 stitch decreased; 38 (44, 50, 54, 60, 60, 60, 60) stitches total.

Decrease Gusset Round 2: k1, sl1yo, BRK, knit to last 2 stitches, p2tog—1 stitch decreased; 37 (43, 49, 53, 59, 59, 59, 59) stitches total.

Repeat Decrease Gusset Round 1 once more—1 stitch decreased; 36 (42, 48, 52, 58, 58, 58, 58) stitches total.

Next Round: k1, sl1yo, BRK, knit to last stitch, end p1.

Next Round: p1, BRP, sl1yo, purl to end.

Repeat last 2 rows 5 more times.

Decrease Round: k1, sl1yo, BRK, k1, k2tog, knit to last 4 stitches, skp, k1, p1—2 stitches decreased; 34 (40, 46, 50, 56, 56, 56, 56) stitches total.

Repeat Decrease Round every 0 (0, 14th, 10th, 6th, 6th, 6th, 6th) row 0 (0, 1, 3, 6, 6, 6, 6) more times—34 (40, 44, 44, 44, 44, 44, 44) stitches.

Work even until Sleeve measures 11½ (11½, 11½, 11½, 12½, 12½, 12½, 12½)" [29 (29, 29, 29, 32, 32, 32, 32) cm] from underarm gusset, ending with a knit row.

Next Round: p1, BRP, sl1yo, purl to end.

Next Round: k2, BRK, knit to last stitch, end p1, remove marker.

Work I-Cord Bind Off as follows: *k2, skp, with yarn in back, slip 3 stitches from the RH needle back to LH needle; repeat from * until all the stitches are worked and 3 stitches remain. Cut 8" [20 cm] of tail and with yarn behind weave tail through remaining stitches to fasten off. Use Seaming Bind Off to Selvedge to join I-Cord edges together.

LEFT SLEEVE

Slip 36 (42, 48, 52, 58, 58, 58, 58) stitches purlwise to 16" [40.5 cm] circular needles. Rejoin new ball of yarn with RS facing and pick up and knit 3 stitches along underarm gusset to close gap, knit to 4 stitches before underarm gusset pick up, k1, BRK, sl1yo, k1, pm for beginning of round—39 (45, 51, 55, 61, 61, 61, 61) stitches.

Decrease Gusset Round 1: p2tog, purl to last 3 stitches, sl1yo, BRP, p1—1 stitch decreased; 38 (44, 50, 54, 60, 60, 60, 60) stitches total.

Decrease Gusset Round 2: p2tog, knit to last 3 stitches, BRK, sl1yo, k1—1 stitch decreased; 37 (43, 49, 53, 59, 59, 59, 59) stitches total.

Repeat Decrease Gusset Round 1 once more—1 stitch decreased; 36 (42, 48, 52, 58, 58, 58, 58) stitches.

Next Round: p1, knit to last 3 stitches, BRK, sl1yo, k1.

Next Round: purl to last 3 stitches, sl1yo, BRP, p1.

Repeat last 2 rows 5 more times.

Decrease Round: p1, k1, k2tog, knit to last 6 stitches, skp, k1, BRK, sl1yo, k1—2 stitches decreased; 34 (40, 46, 50, 56, 56, 56, 56) stitches total.

Repeat Decrease Round every 0 (0, 14th, 10th, 6th, 6th, 6th, 6th) row 0 (0, 1, 3, 6, 6, 6, 6) more times—34 (40, 44, 44, 44, 44, 44, 44) stitches.

Work even until Sleeve measures 11½ (11½, 11½, 11½, 12½, 12½, 12½, 12½)" [29 (29, 29, 29, 32, 32, 32, 32) cm] from underarm gusset, ending with a knit row.

Next Round: purl to last 4 stitches, k2, BRP, p1.

Next Round: p1, knit to last 5 stitches.

Work I-Cord Bind Off as follows, removing marker as you go: *k2, skp, with yarn in back, slip 3 stitches from the RH needle back to LH needle; repeat from * until all stitches are worked and a total of 6 stitches remain. Cut 8" [20 cm] of tail and with yarn behind, weave tail through remaining stitches to fasten off. Use Seaming Bind Off to Selvedge to join I-Cord edges together.

finishing

Weave in all ends. Soak the jacket in cool water using a gentle woolen soap for 10 to 15 minutes. Reshape to final measurement and lay flat to dry. Lightly steam.

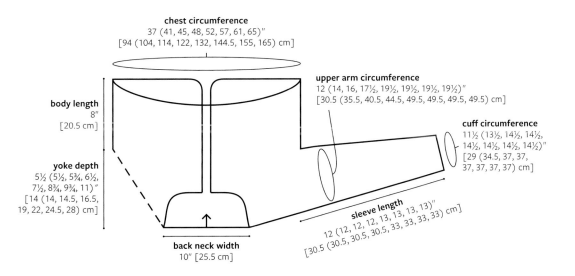

sojourn

sow·jrn

---

noun

a temporary stay

verb

to stay somewhere temporarily

—Sojourner Truth

Truth was a knitter who took her own name. She lived forty years as an enslaved person, then spent the latter forty years of her life free and actively advocating for our rights as an abolitionist and women's rights activist. And for two years at the State University of New York at New Paltz, I got to walk along tree-lined Hawk Drive to the Sojourner Truth Library every day. I entered the building, and it was always an inspiring sight to see a Black woman's likeness etched in metal. Her life is a reminder of how profoundly our circumstances can evolve within just one lifetime. She sparked my interest in the word *sojourn*.

Sojourn as a state of mind.

Sojourn as a permanent rest state.

Sojourn as a respite from suffering.

Sojourn as the gateway to boundless creativity.

Sojourn as moments of noticing.

Sojourn as an acknowledgment to the ephemerality of our lives.

Sojourn as the dates we have with our knitting.

Imagine each project a new city you get to visit from your own home, from a blanket in the park to a train ride to work. And in moments of doubt, there is always a restful place within yourself, a retreat where all things are possible and only peace awaits you.

In almost every portrait I've seen of Truth, she wears a triangular shawl and holds an in-progress project in her lap. The Sojourn Shawl was inspired by this iconic image.

sojourn shawl

begin left side

Using US 4 [3.5 mm] dpns and Long Tail Tubular Cast On, cast on 15 stitches.

Foundation Row 1: *k1tbl, slip 1 purlwise wyif; repeat from * to last stitch, end k1.

Foundation Row 2: slip 1 knitwise wyib, *k1, slip 1 purlwise wyif; repeat from * to last 2 stitches, turn LH dpn clockwise so purl side of the last 2 stitches are facing you, slip 2 purlwise wyif.

Next Row: k3, *p1, k1; repeat from * to last 2 stitches, end slip 2 purlwise wyif.

shape brioche

Note: After working a few rows, place the removable marker to mark the RS of work.

Foundation Row 1 (RS): Change to 24" [60 cm] circular needles size US 7 [4.5 mm], k2, *sl1yo, k1; repeat from * to last 3 stitches, sl1yo, slip 2 purlwise wyif.

Foundation Rows 2 and 4 (WS): k2, [BRK, sl1yo] to last 3 stitches, BRK, slip 2 purlwise wyif.

Foundation Row 3: k2, [sl1yo, BRK] to last 3 stitches, sl1yo, slip 2 purlwise wyif.

INCREASE SECTION 1

Increase Row 1 (RS): k2, sl1yo, [BRK, sl1yo] 2 times, BRKYOBRK, [sl1yo, BRK] to last 3 stitches, sl1yo, slip 2 purlwise wyif—2 stitches increased; 17 stitches total.

Row 2: k2, BRK, [sl1yo, BRK] to last 10 stitches, sl1yo, k1, sl1yo, [BRK, sl1yo] 2 times, BRK, slip 2 purlwise wyif.

Rows 3, 5, and 7: k2, [sl1yo, BRK] to last 3 stitches, sl1yo, slip 2 purlwise wyif.

MATERIALS

4 skeins Purl Soho "Flax Down" (43% baby alpaca, 42% extra-fine merino, 15% linen; 219 yards/ 100 grams) in Oyster Gray, or approximately 870 yards [795 m] of light worsted-weight yarn

24" [60 cm] circular needles size US 7 [4.5 mm]

Double pointed needles size US 4 [3.5 mm]

Removable stitch marker

Tapestry needle

Scissors

GAUGE

17 stitches and 40 rows = 4" [10 cm] over brioche stitch using US 7 [4.5 mm] needles or size needed to obtain gauge

Note: When counting brioche rows, each knit stitch in a column represents 2 rows.

FINISHED MEASUREMENTS

Wingspan, cast on edge to cast on edge: approx. 50" [127 cm]

Length along I-Cord seam: 27" [68 cm]

Rows 4, 6, and 8: k2, [BRK, sl1yo] to last 3 stitches, BRK, slip 2 purlwise wyif.

Repeat Increase Row 1 to Row 8 of Increase Section 1 two more times—21 stitches.

INCREASE SECTION 2

Increase Row 1 (RS): k2, sl1yo, [BRK, sl1yo] 2 times, BRKYOBRK, [sl1yo, BRK] to last 7 stitches, sl1yo, BRKYOBRK, sl1yo, BRK, sl1yo, slip 2 purlwise wyif—4 stitches increased; 25 stitches total.

Row 2: k2, BRK, sl1yo, BRK, sl1yo, k1, sl1yo, [BRK, sl1yo] to last 9 stitches, k1, [sl1yo, BRK] 3 times, slip 2 purlwise wyif.

Rows 3, 5, and 7: k2, [sl1yo, BRK] to last 3 stitches, sl1yo, slip 2 purlwise wyif.

Rows 4, 6, and 8: k2, [BRK, sl1yo] to last 3 stitches, BRK, slip 2 purlwise wyif.

Repeat Rows 1 to 8 of Increase Section 2 for 23 more times—117 stitches.

German Short Row 1 (RS): k2, [sl1yo, BRK] 45 times to last 25 stitches, pm, turn and make double stitch, [BRK, sl1yo] 44 times to last 3 stitches, BRK, slip 2 purlwise wyif.

German Short Row 2 (RS): k2, [sl1yo, BRK] 44 times to 2 stitches before last wrap, turn and make double stitch, [BRK, sl1yo] 43 times to last 3 stitches, BRK, slip 2 purlwise wyif.

German Short Row 3 (RS): k2, [sl1yo, BRK] to 2 stitches before last wrap, turn and make double stitch, [BRK, sl1yo] to last 3 stitches, BRK, slip 2 purlwise wyif.

Repeat German Short Row 3 for 36 more times.

Last German Short Row (RS): k2, [sl1yo, BRK] 6 times to 2 stitches before last wrap, turn and make double stitch, [BRK, sl1yo] 5 times to last 3 stitches, BRK, slip 2 purlwise wyif.

Next Row (RS): k2, [sl1yo, BRK] to last 3 stitches, removing marker, sl1yo, slip 2 purlwise wyif.

Next Row: k2, [BRK, sl1yo] to last 3 stitches, BRK, slip 2 purlwise wyif.

Next Row: k2, [p1, BRK] to last 3 stitches, removing marker, p1, slip 2 purlwise wyif.

Work I-Cord Bind Off as follows: *k1, skp, with yarn in back, slip 2 stitches from RH needle back to LH needle; repeat from * until 4 stitches remain, ending last repeat with skp. You will have 2 stitches on each needle. Using Kitchener Stitch, join I-Cord Selvedge stitches together. Cut 8" [20 cm] of tail.

begin right side

Using US 4 [3.5 mm] dpns and Long Tail Tubular Cast On, cast on 15 stitches.

Foundation Row 1: *k1tbl, slip 1 purlwise wyif; repeat from * to last stitch, k1.

Foundation Row 2: slip 1 knitwise wyib, *k1, slip 1 purlwise wyif; repeat from * to last 2 stitches, turn left hand dpn clockwise so purl sides of last 2 stitches are facing you, slip 2 purlwise wyif.

Next Row: k3, *p1, k1; repeat from * to last 2 stitches, slip 2 purlwise wyif.

shape brioche

Note: After working a few rows, place the removable marker to mark the RS of work.

Foundation Row 1 (RS): Change to 24" [60 cm] circular needles size US 7 [4.5 mm], k2, *sllyo, k1; repeat from * to last 3 stitches, sllyo, slip 2 purlwise wyif.

Foundation Rows 2 and 4 (WS): k2, [BRK, sllyo] to last 3 stitches, BRK, slip 2 purlwise wyif.

Foundation Row 3: k2, [sllyo, BRK] to last 3 stitches, sllyo, slip 2 purlwise wyif.

INCREASE SECTION 1

Increase Row 1 (RS): k2, sllyo, [BRK, sllyo] 2 times, BRKYOBRK, [sllyo, BRK] 2 times, sllyo, slip 2 purlwise wyif— 2 stitches increased; 17 stitches total.

Row 2: k2, BRK, [sllyo, BRK] 2 times, sllyo, k1, sllyo, [BRK, sllyo] to last 3 stitches, BRK, slip 2 purlwise wyif.

Rows 3, 5, and 7: k2, [sllyo, BRK] to last 3 stitches, sllyo, slip 2 purlwise wyif.

Rows 4, 6, and 8: k2, [BRK, sllyo] to last 3 stitches, BRK, slip 2 purlwise wyif.

Increase Row 9: k2, sllyo, [BRK, sllyo] to last 8 stitches, BRKYOBRK, [sllyo, BRK] 2 times, sllyo, slip 2 purlwise wyif.

Repeat Row 2 to Increase Row 9 of Increase Section 1 once, then repeat Row 2 to Row 8 once more—21 stitches.

INCREASE SECTION 2

Increase Row 1 (RS): k2, sl1yo, BRK, sl1yo, BRKYOBRK, [sl1yo, BRK] to last 9 stitches, sl1yo, BRKYOBRK, [sl1yo, BRK] 2 times, sl1yo, slip 2 purlwise wyif—4 stitches increased; 25 stitches total.

Row 2 (WS): k2, BRK, [sl1yo, BRK] 2 times, sl1yo, k1, sl1yo, [BRK, sl1yo] to last 7 stitches, k1, [sl1yo, BRK] 2 times, slip 2 purlwise wyif.

Rows 3, 5, and 7: k2, [sl1yo, BRK] to last 3 stitches, sl1yo, slip 2 purlwise wyif.

Rows 4, 6, and 8: k2, [BRK, sl1yo] to last 3 stitches, BRK, slip 2 purlwise wyif.

Repeat Increase Row 1 to Row 8 of Increase Section 2 for 23 more times, ending last repeat with Row 7—117 stitches.

german short rows

German Short Row 1 (WS): k2, BRK, [sl1yo, BRK] 45 times to last 24 stitches, pm, turn and make double stitch, [BRK, sl1yo] 45 times to last 2 stitches, slip 2 purlwise wyif.

German Short Row 2 (WS): k2, BRK, [sl1yo, BRK] 44 times to 2 stitches before last turn, turn and make double stitch, [BRK, sl1yo] 44 times to last 2 stitches, slip 2 purlwise wyif.

German Short Row 3 (WS): k2, BRK, [sl1yo, BRK] to 2 stitches before last turn, turn and make double stitch, [BRK, sl1yo] to last 2 stitches, slip 2 purlwise wyif.

Repeat German Short Row 3 for 36 more times.

Last German Short Row (WS): k2, BRK, [sl1yo, BRK] 6 times, turn and make double stitch, [BRK, sl1yo] 6 times to last 2 stitches, slip 2 purlwise wyif.

Next Row (WS): k2, BRK, [sl1yo, BRK] to last 2 stitches, slip 2 purlwise wyif.

Next Row: k2, [p1, BRK] to last 3 stitches, p1, slip 2 purlwise wyif.

Work I-Cord Bind-Off as follows: *k1, skp, with yarn in back, slip 2 stitches from RH needle back to LH needle; repeat from * until 4 stitches remain, ending last repeat with skp. You will have 2 stitches on each needle. Using Kitchener Stitch, join I-Cord Selvedge stitches together. Cut 3 yards [3 m] of tail for sewing the seam.

finishing

SEAMING

Lay both sides flat with WS facing so that the I-Cord Bind Off edges are side by side. Using Seaming Bind Off to Bind Off and long sewing tail, join the two sides together, sewing right below the I-Cord Bind Off and between I-Cord Selvedge edges. The I-Cord Bind Off edges will fall to the RS of the work to create the piping along the back.

WASH AND BLOCK

Weave in all ends. Soak the shawl in cool water using a gentle woolen soap for 10 to 15 minutes. Reshape and lay flat to dry.

dawn

dän

---

noun

the first appearance of light in the sky before sunrise

the beginning of a phenomenon or period of time,
especially one considered favorable

verb

to come into existence

to become evident to the mind; be perceived
or understood

"YOU'VE GOT TO WRITE YOUR OWN WORLDS. YOU'VE GOT TO WRITE YOURSELF IN."

—Octavia Butler

When I read Butler's books, I must slow down. Savor them a little. Her pages are especially fragrant—they almost seem to sparkle. The characters are dark and attractive. I am reading the Xenogenesis series for the third time, beginning with *Dawn*. Lilith Iyapo awakens from 250 years of sleep on a vast Oankali spaceship, where dinner is served within pseudo trees and the people have saved her from a scorched world. She is evolving, resistant to the change, and being prepared to lead humans back to our healed earth. Awakenings can happen after years or after a short nap. There is no gender binary and the third gender, the ooloi, have the ability to alter and merge DNA.

I love how the Oankali say no. No, period. When you persist, their tentacles go limp and they disengage from the conversation. Silence. I've talked about the art of saying yes. But no is equally important. My no has been trained out of me since infancy. I'm doing GI Jane training trying to get it back. It takes daily practice. It's not easy. I must be subversive. Direct. Persistent. And every time I thoughtfully say no to an energy exchange—sometimes reciprocal, sometimes not—my personal commitment to take better care of myself for myself, my loved ones, and my communities is like a profound awakening, a new day.

Work toward the casual naming of your boundaries, hopes, and expectations, no matter the audience, because when we take better care of ourselves we are more capable of taking care of each other. A flourishing world is awaiting us if only we can stop to listen. Arundhati Roy said, "Another world is not only possible, she is on her way. On a quiet day, I can hear her breathing."

The Dawn Cowl is about the full-hearted *yes*, our possibility. The beginning of the round changes throughout the pattern. You will shift the marker as the objective changes. It can feel confusing at times, and that's a natural feeling. Lean into it. Follow the instructions. Trust in your ability to begin again, to awaken in a new world of your own making. And remember to say *no* when you need to—no, I will not be distracted; no, I will not change course; no, I will not stop trying.

Do you see them? The lungs on Dawn? I do. And I remember how to breathe.

dawn cowl

double knit edge

Using 24" [60 cm] circular needles size US 11 [8 mm] and Long Tail Tubular Cast On, CO 99 stitches.

Row 1 (RS): *k1tbl, slip 1 purlwise wyif; repeat from * to last stitch, k1.

Row 2: p1, *k1, slip 1 purlwise wyif; repeat from * to last 2 stitches, k1, p1.

Row 3: *k1, slip 1 purlwise wyif; repeat from * to last stitch, k1.

Change to 24" [60 cm] circular needles size US 13 [9 mm]. Repeat last 2 rows 3 more times.

shape shoulder

Foundation Row (WS): p8, k2, pm, p14, pm, p51, pm, p14, pm, k2, p8.

Row 1 (RS): knit to 4 stitches before marker, LLI, k1, p2, slm, k1, skp, knit to 2 stitches before next marker, k2tog, slm, k6, skp, knit to 8 stitches before next marker, k2tog, k6, slm, skp, knit to 3 stitches before next marker, k2tog, k1, slm, p2, k1, RLI, knit to end—6 stitches decreased; 2 stitches increased; 95 stitches total.

Row 2: knit the knits and purl the purls, slipping all markers.

Repeat last 2 rows 3 more times. DO NOT TURN at end of last WS row—83 stitches.

With WS facing and using Thumb Cast On, cast 6 stitches onto the RH needle—89 stitches. Turn to RS.

Note: Change to 16" [40.5 cm] circular needles size US 13 [8 mm] when there are too few stitches to work comfortably on the longer needle.

Joining Round: k18, p2, slm, k1, skp, k1, k2tog, slm, k6, skp, knit to 8 stitches before next marker, k2tog, k6, slm, skp,

MATERIALS

3 skeins Ocean by the Sea "Thicc" (100% merino wool; 76 yards/100 grams) in Caramel or approximately 228 yards [210 m] of chunky-weight yarn

24" [60 cm] circular needles size US 10½ [6.5 mm]

16" [40.5 cm] and 24" [60 cm] circular needles size US 11 [8 mm]

16" [40.5 cm] and 24" [60 cm] circular needles size US 13 [9 mm]

Double pointed needles size US 10 [6 mm]

Crochet hook size US G-6 [4 mm]

Stitch markers

Scrap yarn

Scissors

Tapestry needle

GAUGE

11 stitches and 13 rows = 4" [10 cm] over Stockinette Stitch using US 13 [9 mm] needles or size needed to obtain gauge

FINISHED MEASUREMENTS

Circumference at neck edge: 26" [66 cm]

Width along cast on edge at shoulder: 36" [91.5 cm]

Length at center back: 19" [48 cm]

k1, k2tog, k1, slm, p2, k11, k2tog (knit the last stitch on the RH needle together with the first stitch on the LH needle to join the round), k2, pm to mark center front, k2, skp, knit to 2 stitches before next marker, p2, pm of contrasting color to mark beginning of round—8 stitches decreased; 81 stitches total.

Note: Continue to slip all markers unless otherwise noted to remove or replace with a contrasting color. There will be many new beginnings.

Rounds 1, 3, and 5: knit the knits and purl the purls to 4 stitches before center front marker, k2tog, k2, slm, k2, skp, knit to last 2 stitches, p2—2 stitches decreased.

Round 2: k2, k2tog, slm, k6, skp, knit to 8 stitches before next marker, k2tog, k6, slm, skp, k2, slm, p2, knit to 4 stitches before center front marker, k2tog, k2, slm, k2, skp, knit to last 2 stitches, p2— 6 stitches decreased; 73 stitches total.

Round 4: k1, k2tog, slm, k6, skp, knit to 8 stitches before next marker, k2tog, k6, slm, skp, k1, slm, p2, knit to 4 stitches before center front marker, k2tog, k2, slm, k2, skp, knit to last 2 stitches, p2— 6 stitches decreased; 65 stitches total.

Round 6: k2tog, slm, k6, skp, knit to 8 stitches before next marker, k2tog, k6, slm, skp, slm, p2, knit to 4 stitches before center front marker, k2tog, k2, slm, k2, skp, knit to last 2 stitches, p2—6 stitches decreased; 57 stitches total.

Round 7: knit the knits and purl the purls to 4 stitches before center front marker, k2tog, k2, slm, k2, skp, knit to last 2 stitches, p2—2 stitches decreased; 55 stitches total.

make crochet seams

Note: Crochet seams (see page 58) are worked on either side of the purl ribs to tighten neighboring stitches and create structure.

Round 1: remove beginning marker, turn to WS, *using crochet hook, create a crochet seam between the needles next to the knit stitch beginning just above the Double-Knit Edge, place seam stitch onto the RH needle purlwise and turn to RS of work*, with working yarn, k2tog (knit next stitch together with seam stitch), pm of contrasting color for new beginning of round, k6, skp, knit to 8 stitches before next marker, k2tog, k6, slm, slip 1 knitwise, remove marker; repeat from * to * once more, with working yarn, k1 seam stitch, pass the slipped stitch over, p2, knit to 4 stitches before center marker, k2tog, k2, slm, k2, skp, knit to last 3 stitches, p1, k2tog—5 stitches decreased; 50 stitches total.

Round 2: knit to marker, slm, skp, p1, knit to 4 stitches before center front marker, k2tog, k2, slm, k2, skp, knit to last 2 stitches, k2tog—4 stitches decreased; 46 stitches total.

Round 3: k6, skp, knit to 8 stitches before next marker, k2tog, k6, slm, skp, k1, k2tog, k2, slm, k2, skp, k1, turn to WS, create a crochet seam between the needles next to the knit stitch beginning just above the Double-Knit Edge, place seam stitch onto the RH needle purlwise and turn to RS, with working yarn, k2tog (knit next stitch together with seam stitch)—5 stitches decreased; 41 stitches total.

Round 4: knit to next marker, remove marker, slip 1 knitwise, turn to WS, create a crochet seam between the needles next to the knit stitch beginning just above the Double-Knit Edge, place seam stitch onto the RH needle purlwise and turn to RS, with working yarn, k1 seam stitch, pass the slipped stitch over, k2tog, k2, slm, k2, skp, k1, remove beginning marker, k13, pm, k5, pm of contrasting color to mark new beginning of round—2 stitches decreased; 5 stitches at center back between markers; 17 stitches each side of center front marker; 39 stitches total.

shape neck

Change to 16" [40.5 cm] circular needles size US 11 [8 mm].

Next Round: knit to 4 stitches before center front marker, k2tog, k2, slm, k2, skp, knit to end—2 stitches decreased; 37 stitches total.

Repeat last round once more—35 stitches.

Knit 4 rounds even.

Change to 16" [40.5 cm] circular needles size US 13 [9 mm].

Increase Rounds 1 and 3: knit to 3 stitches before center front marker, m1L, k3, slm, k3, m1R, knit to end—2 stitches increased.

Rounds 2 and 4: knit.

Increase Round 5: knit to 3 stitches before center front marker, m1L, k3, slm, k3, m1R, knit to next marker, slm, LLI, knit to last stitch, RLI—4 stitches increased; 43 stitches total.

Round 6: knit.

Repeat last 2 rounds 5 more times—63 stitches.

shape head

Change to 24" [60 cm] circular needles size US 11 [8 mm].

Next Increase Round: Knit to last marker, slm, LLI, knit to last stitch, RLI—2 stitches increased; 65 stitches total.

WRAP & TURN SHORT ROWS
Short Row 1 (RS): knit to 4 stitches before center front marker, W&T, purl to 4 stitches before center front marker, W&T.

Short Row 2 (RS): knit to next marker, slm, LLI, knit to 1 stitch before beginning marker, RLI, slm, knit to 2 stitches before previous wrap, W&T, purl to 2 stitches before previous wrap, W&T—2 stitches increased; 67 stitches total.

Repeat Short Row 2 two more times—71 stitches.

Next Short Row (RS): knit to 2 stitches before previous wrap, W&T, purl to 2 stitches before previous wrap, W&T.

Next Short Row (RS): knit to 2 stitches before previous wrap, W&T, purl to 2 stitches before previous wrap, W&T, knit to beginning marker.

Change to 24" [60 cm] circular needles size US 10½ [6.5 mm].

Next Round: k8, [k1, pick up wrap] 6 times, k3, remove marker, k3, [pick up wrap, k1] 6 times, k8, remove marker, k25.

knit hem

Work Knit Hem Bind Off as follows: Knit 1 round. Weave a lifeline using a contrasting color into the row below to mark the hemline. Knit 10 more rounds. Remove marker. Turn cowl inside out. Cut 2 yards [2 m] of sewing tail and thread it onto a tapestry needle.

Joining Row (WS): Fold the hem down and in half so the knit side is facing and the live stitches are lined up along the lifeline. Being sure to join live stitch with corresponding lifeline stitch below, *insert tapestry needle up and under the purl bump just above the lifeline, insert tapestry needle knitwise into next live stitch on needle and drop off the needle, pull yarn taut; repeat from * until all live stitches are joined to the WS of cowl. Remove lifeline.

finishing

APPLIED I-CORD EDGE
With WS of cowl facing, attach an I-Cord along the bottom center front of cowl as follows: using US 10 [6 mm] dpns. *k2, slip 1 knitwise, pick up and k1 along bottom center front, pass the slipped stitch over, do not turn, bring yarn behind; repeat from *, picking up into every available space along the selvedge edge. Cut 6" [15 cm] of tail and weave through remaining 3 stitches to fasten off.

WASH AND BLOCK
Weave in all ends. Soak the cowl in cool water using a gentle woolen soap for 10 to 15 minutes. Reshape and lay flat to dry. Lightly steam block to final measurements.

joie

joi

---

noun

exuberant enjoyment of life; a feeling of great
pleasure and happiness

verb

rejoice

"MY MIND IS POWERFUL. MY MAGIC IS STRONG. IT IS IRRESPONSIBLE TO VISUALIZE THAT WHICH I DO NOT WANT TO MANIFEST. TREAT YOURSELF AS IF YOU ARE VALUABLE. AS IF YOUR LIFE IS A SACRED, PRECIOUS THING."

—Jamila Reddy

There is no need to wait. Your joy is always present, awaiting you.

A series of honest declarations create a container to sincerely express our happiness and discontentment. Joy allows us to experience gratefulness and longing, grief and hopefulness, cradling them with both hands.

Alice Walker says, "Laughter isn't even the other side of tears, it is tears turned inside out."

The interlocking cables of Joie give us permission to be joyous in our ability to feel it all.

These mittens are delightfully repetitive, the cables branching out in groups of three. Let's imagine one stitch represents a pleasurable emotion; it spikes our endorphins and makes us laugh. The second pulls at our hearts and minds, calling for us to take notice. The third stitch is a careful balance of encouraging one to feed the other until we feel fulfilled.

Joy is always present, hands open, waiting for you.

joie mittens

left mitten

CUFF

Using Long Tail Cast On and US 6 [4 mm] dpns, CO 50 (54) stitches onto Needle 1. Do not turn. Beginning at RS of needle, divide stitches onto dpns as follows: Slip 10 (12) stitches onto Needle 2, 15 stitches onto Needle 3, 15 stitches onto Needle 4.

Joining Round: pm to mark beginning of round on Needle 1, work next 10 (12) stitches from Needle 2 to Needle 1 to place beginning of round at the center of Needle 1 as follows: p1 to join round, being careful not to twist stitches, k6 (8), p3; continue the rest of the round using dpns normally as follows: k30, p3, k6 (8), p1.

Note: Work with a total of 4 dpns; there are 20 (24) stitches on Needle 1, 15 stitches each on Needles 2 and 3, and the 4th dpn is for working in the round. Rounds begin at the center of Needle 1. (See page 57 for working in the round on dpns.)

Round 1: p1, k6 (8), p3, k30, p3, k6 (8), p1.

Round 2 and following even rounds: p1, k6 (8), p3, k30, p3, k6 (8), p1.

Round 3: p1, k6 (8), p3, k9, C6B, C6F, k9, p3, k6 (8), p1.

Round 5: p1, k6 (8), p3, k6, C6B, k6, C6F, k6, p3, k6 (8), p1.

Round 7: p1, k6 (8), p3, k3, C6B, k12, C6F, k3, p3, k6 (8), p1.

Round 9: p1, k6 (8), p3, C6B, k18, C6F, p3, k6 (8), p1.

Round 10: Repeat Round 2.

SHAPE LEFT THUMB GUSSET

Round 1: p1, k2, LLI, k1, RLI, k1 (3), p3, k9, C6B, C6F, k9, p3, k6 (8), p1—2 stitches increased.

Round 2: p1, k8 (10), p3, k30, p3, k6, p1.

Round 3: p1, k2, LLI, k3, RLI, k1 (3), p3, k6, C6B, k6, C6F, k6, p3, k6, p1—2 stitches increased.

MATERIALS

1 skein Purl Soho "Flax Down" (43% baby alpaca, 42% extra-fine merino, 15% linen; 219 yards/100 grams) in Steel Blue or approximately 190 (220) yards [174 (202) m] of light worsted-weight yarn

Double pointed needles size US 3 [3.75 mm]

8" [20 cm] long set of 4 double pointed needles size US 6 [4 mm]

Crochet hook size US B-1 [2.25 mm]

Cable needle

Removable stitch marker

Stitch holders or scrap yarn

Tapestry needle

Scissors

GAUGE

22 stitches and 32 rounds = 4" [10 cm] over Stockinette Stitch using US 6 [4 mm] needles or size to obtain gauge

FINISHED MEASUREMENTS

Cuff circumference: 9 (9¾)" [23 (24.5) cm]

Total length along center front: 10 (11)" [25.5 (28) cm]

CABLE STITCH PATTERN

This cable is worked over 30 stitches across the top of the mittens. Row-by-row instructions for the cable are written out in each round, and you can also reference the chart.

C6B: Cable 6 Back: slip 3 stitches to cn, hold to back, k3, k3 from cn.

C6F: Cable 6 Front: slip 3 stitches to cn, hold to front, k3, k3 from cn.

Round 4 and following even rounds: knit the knits and purl the purls as established.

Round 5: p1, k2, LLI, k5, RLI, k1 (3), p3, k3, C6B, k12, C6F, k3, p3, k6, p1—2 stitches increased.

Round 7: p1, k2, LLI, k7, RLI, k1 (3), p3, C6B, k18, C6F, p3, k6, p1—2 stitches increased.

Round 9: p1, k2, LLI, k9, RLI, k1 (3), p3, k9, C6B, C6F, k9, p3, k6, p1—2 stitches increased.

Round 11: p1, k2, LLI, skp, k7, k2tog, RLI, k1 (3), p3, k6, C6B, k6, C6F, k6, p3, k6, p1.

Round 12 and following even rounds: p1, k16 (18), p3, k30, p3, k6 (8), p1.

Round 13: p1, k2, LLI, k1, skp, k5, k2tog, k1, RLI, k1 (3), p3, k3, C6B, k12, C6F, k3, p3, k6, p1.

Round 15: p1, k2, LLI, k2, skp, k3, k2tog, k2, RLI, k1 (3), p3, C6B, k18, C6F, p3, k6, p1.

Round 17: p1, k2, LLI, k3, skp, k1, k2tog, k3, RLI, k1 (3), p3, k9, C6B, C6F, k9, p3, k6, p1.

SEPARATE LEFT THUMB GUSSET FROM HAND

Round 19: p1, k2, slip 13 stitches onto stitch holder, CO 3 stitches using Thumb Cast On, k1 (3), p3, k6, C6B, k6, C6F, k6, p3, k6, p1—50 (54) stitches.

Round 20: p1, k6 (8), p3, k30, p3, k6 (8), p1.

SHAPE HAND

Increase Round 1: p1, k6 (8), p3, m1p, k3, C6B, k12, C6F, k3, m1p, p3, k6 (8), p1—2 stitches increased; 52 (56) stitches total.

Round 2 and following even rounds: p1, k6 (8), p4, k30, p4, k6 (8), p1.

Round 3: p1, k6 (8), p4, C6B, k18, C6F, p4, k6 (8), p1.

Round 5: p1, k6 (8), p4, k9, C6B, C6F, k9, p4, k6 (8), p1.

Round 7: p1, k6 (8), p4, k6, C6B, k6, C6F, k6, p4, k6 (8), p1.

Round 9: p1, k6 (8), p4, k3, C6B, k12, C6F, k3, p4, k6 (8), p1.

Round 11: p1, k6 (8), p4, C6B, k18, C6F, p4, k6 (8), p1.

Round 12: p1, k6 (8), p4, k30, p4, k6 (8), p1.

Repeat Rounds 5 to 12 for 3 (4) more times, ending last repeat with Round 11.

MAKE CROCHET SEAMS

Next Round: p1, k6 (8), p4, *turn mitten WS out, using crochet hook, create a crochet seam (see page 58) next to the cable and between the needles beginning just above CO edge, place seam stitch onto RH needle purlwise and turn mitten RS out,* with working yarn, k2tog (knit next stitch together with seam stitch), k28, slip 1 knitwise, repeat from * to * once, with working yarn, k1 seam stitch, psso, p4, k6 (8), p1.

SHAPE TOP

Redistribute stitches over dpns, slipping 4 Reverse Stockinette stitches on each side of the cable onto cable dpns. Each cable dpn (Needles 2 and 3) has 19 stitches, and remaining needle has 14 (18) stitches.

Decrease Round 1: p1, k6 (8), p4, k8, slip 4 to cable needle and hold behind, k3, [k2tog, k2] from cable needle, slip 3 to cable needle and hold in front, k2, skp, k3 from cable needle, k8, p4, k6 (8), p1—2 stitches decreased; 50 (54) stitches total.

Decrease Round 2: p1, k6 (8), p4, k3, k2tog, k18, skp, k3, p4, k6 (8), p1—2 stitches decreased; 48 (52) stitches total.

Decrease Round 3: p1, k6 (8), p3, k2tog, k2, slip 4 to cable needle and hold behind, k3, [k2tog, k2] from cable needle, k6, slip 3 to cable needle and hold in front, k2, skp, k3 from cable needle, k2, skp, p3, k6 (8), p1—4 stitches decreased; 44 (48) stitches total.

Decrease Round 4: p1, k6 (8), p3, k6, k2tog, k8, skp, k6, p3, k6 (8), p1—2 stitches decreased; 42 (46) stitches total.

Decrease Round 5: p1, k6 (8), p3, C6B, k2tog, k6, skp, C6F, p3, k6 (8), p1—2 stitches decreased; 40 (44) stitches total.

Decrease Round 6: p1, k3, skp, k1 (3), p2, k2tog, k2, k2tog, k10, skp, k2, skp, p2, k1 (3), k2tog, k3, p1—6 stitches decreased; 34 (38) stitches total.

Decrease Round 7: p1, k2, skp, k1 (3), p2, k3, C6B, C6F, k3, p2, k1 (3), k2tog, k2, p1—2 stitches decreased; 32 (36) stitches total.

Decrease Round 8: p1, k1, skp, k1 (3), p2, k6, [k2tog] 3 times, k6, p2, k1 (3), k2tog, k1, p1—5 stitches decreased; 27 (31) stitches total.

Decrease Round 9: p1, k1, k2tog, k0 (2), p2, slip 3 to cable needle and hold in back, k3, k2tog from cable needle, slip last stitch on cable needle to LH needle, k2tog, k1, slip 1 knitwise onto RH needle, slip 3 to cable needle and hold in front, k1, psso, skp, k3 from cable needle, p2, k0 (2), skp, k1, p1—6 stitches decreased; 21 (25) stitches total.

Decrease Round 10: p1, k2tog, k0 (2), p1, k2tog, k1, skp, s2kp, k2tog, k1, skp, p1, k0 (2), skp, p1—8 stitches decreased; 13 (17) stitches total.

Change to US 3 [3.25 mm] dpns.

Decrease Round 11: [k2tog] 3 (4) times, k1, [skp] 3 (4) times—7 (9) stitches.

Cut 8" [20 cm] of tail and thread through remaining stitches. Keep tail to fasten off live crochet seam stitches during finishing.

MAKE LEFT THUMB
Slip 13 stitches onto two US 6 [4 mm] dpns. Using 3rd dpn and with RS facing, rejoin yarn, k13, pick up and knit 7 stitches along thumb gusset gap—20 stitches.

Pm to mark beginning of round.

Round 1: k12, skp, k4, k2tog—2 stitches decreased; 18 stitches total.

Round 2: k12, skp, k2, k2tog—2 stitches decreased; 16 stitches total.

Round 3: knit.

Work 15 rounds even in Stockinette Stitch.

Change to US 3 [3.25 mm] dpns.

Next round: [k2tog] until 5 stitches remain.

Cut 8" [20 cm] of tail and weave through remaining stitches to fasten off.

right mitten

Work as for Left Mitten through Round 10 of Cuff.

SHAPE RIGHT THUMB GUSSET
Round 1: p1, k6 (8), p3, k9, C6B, C6F, k9, p3, k1 (3), LLI, k1, RLI, k2, p1.

Round 2: p1, k6 (8), p3, k30, p3, k8 (10), p1.

Round 3: p1, k6 (8), p3, k6, C6B, k6, C6F, k6, p3, k1 (3), LLI, k3, RLI, k2, p1.

Round 4 and following even rounds: knit the knits and purl the purls as established.

Round 5: p1, k6 (8), p3, k3, C6B, k12, C6F, k3, p3, k1 (3), LLI, k5, RLI, k2, p1.

Round 7: p1, k6 (8), p3, C6B, k18, C6F, p3, k1 (3), LLI, k7, RLI, k2, p1.

Round 9: p1, k6 (8), p3, k9, C6B, C6F, k9, p3, k1 (3), LLI, k9, RLI, k2, p1.

Round 11: p1, k6 (8), p3, k6, C6B, k6, C6F, k6, p3, k1 (3), LLI, skp, k7, k2tog, RLI, k2, p1.

Round 13: p1, k6 (8), p3, k3, C6B, k12, C6F, k3, p3, k1 (3), LLI, k1, skp, k5, k2tog, k1, RLI, k2, p1.

Round 15: p1, k6 (8), p3, C6B, k18, C6F, p3, k1 (3), LLI, k2, skp, k3, k2tog, k2, RLI, k2, p1.

Round 17: p1, k6 (8), p3, k9, C6B, C6F, k9, p3, k1 (3), LLI, k3, skp, k1, k2tog, k3, RLI, k2, p1.

SEPARATE RIGHT THUMB GUSSET FROM HAND

Round 19: p1, k6 (8), p3, k6, C6B, k6, C6F, k6, p3, k1 (3), slip 13 stitches onto stitch holder, CO 3 stitches using Thumb Cast On, k2, p1—50 (54) stitches.

Round 20: p1, k6 (8), p3, k30, p3, k6 (8), p1.

Beginning with Shape Hand, complete as for Left Mitten.

MAKE RIGHT THUMB

Slip 13 stitches onto two US 6 [4 mm] dpns. Rejoin yarn and pick up and knit 7 stitches along Thumb Gusset gap, then k13 Thumb stitches—20 stitches. Complete as for Left Thumb.

finishing

CROCHET SEAMS FOR RIGHT AND LEFT MITTEN

Turn mittens WS out so the thumb is facing you.

Working from left to right and beginning just above cast on edge, make one crochet seam along each side of the knit stitches at center back and another crochet seam to the left of the cable next to the set of 6 (8) purl stitches. Secure the seam stitches with the top tail.

CRAB STITCH

Using the crochet hook and with WS facing, work 1 row of Crab Stitch along the cast on edge.

WASH AND BLOCK

Weave in all ends. Soak the mitts in cool water using a gentle woolen soap for 10 to 15 minutes. Reshape and lay flat to dry.

JOIE CABLE PATTERN

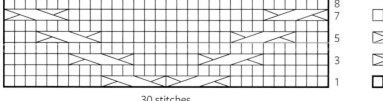

30 stitches

KEY

☐	knit
◁▷	C6B
✕	C6F
☐	pattern repeat

ode

ōd

---

noun

a lyric poem in the form of an address to a
particular subject, often elevated in style or manner
and written in varied or irregular meter

a poem meant to be sung

"STYLE HAS A PROFOUND MEANING TO BLACK AMERICANS.
IF WE CAN'T DRIVE, WE WILL INVENT WALKS, AND THE WORLD
WILL ENVY THE DEXTERITY OF OUR FEET. IF WE CAN'T HAVE
HAM, WE WILL BOIL CHITTERLINGS; IF WE ARE GIVEN ROTTEN
PEACHES, WE WILL MAKE COBBLERS; IF GIVEN SCRAPS, WE WILL
MAKE QUILTS; TAKE AWAY OUR DRUMS, AND WE WILL CLAP
OUR HANDS. WE PROVE THE HUMAN SPIRIT WILL PREVAIL.
WE WILL TAKE WHAT WE HAVE TO MAKE WHAT WE NEED. WE
NEED CONFIDENCE IN OUR KNOWLEDGE OF WHO WE ARE."

—Nikki Giovanni

May I borrow from your abundance?
To build the home I want to see.
To be the garden I'd like to eat.
Create the human I dream to be.
Remind me.
I have everything I need.
I carry all the keys.
You are revolutionary.
Who me?
Walk in your freedom.
I'll see.
You are revolutionary.
Who me?
Yes.
Glorify it, trust me.
Every day is a practice of breaking
*   the chains.*
You'll see.

These lyrics are from a collection of prayers I wrote and workshopped with an incredible group of people in a QTPOC writing workshop led by my dear friend Jamila Reddy in the summer of 2018. There is a cadence when you read it out loud. These words are for you as much as they are for me. A reminder, a prayer, a remembering, a celebration of self.

A familiar style with its raglan lines, shawl collar, and pockets, the Ode Cardigan pays homage to the extraordinary. The color of this piece is called Wura Patina; *wura* is Yoruba for golden.

ode cardigan

body

Work I-Cord Cast On as follows: using Crochet Chain Provisional Cast On, crochet hook, and scrap yarn, make a slipknot and chain 5 stitches. Cut 4" [10 cm] of tail. Fasten off. Using US 11 [8 mm] dpns and main yarn, pick up and knit 3 stitches into the back loops of the crochet chain beginning at the slipknot end. Work I-Cord for 84 (94, 106, 116, 128, 138, 150, 160, 172) rows. Slip 3 working stitches onto 40" [60 cm] circular needles. Pick up and knit 82 (92, 104, 114, 126, 136, 148, 158, 170) stitches into the top half of the first stitch of each row along the I-Cord. Carefully pull the loop and remove the scrap yarn from the provisional cast on. Slip the 3 live stitches onto the RH needle with the purl side facing you with working yarn in front—88 (98, 110, 120, 132, 142, 154, 164, 176) stitches.

Next Row (WS): k3, sl1yo, p15 (18, 21, 23, 26, 29, 32, 34, 37), pm, p50 (54, 60, 66, 72, 76, 82, 88, 94), pm, purl to last 4 stitches, sl1yo, slip 3 purlwise wyif.

Note: Slip all markers.

Increase Row (RS): k3, BRK, LLI, knit to last 5 stitches, RLI, BRK, slip 3 purlwise wyif—2 stitches increased.

Next Row: k3, sl1yo, purl to last 4 stitches, sl1yo, slip 3 purlwise wyif.

Repeat last 2 rows twice more—94 (104, 116, 126, 138, 148, 160, 170, 182) stitches.

BEGIN POCKETS

Increase Row (RS): k3, BRK, LLI, k1, *slip next 15 (15, 15, 15, 17, 17, 19, 19, 21) stitches purlwise onto scrap yarn, with working yarn, working behind held stitches, pick up and knit 15 (15, 15, 15, 17, 17, 19, 19, 21) stitches in the row below the stitches on hold*, knit to last marker, k1 (4, 7, 9, 10, 13, 14, 16, 17), repeat from * to * one more time, k1, RLI, BRK, slip 3 purlwise wyif—2 stitches increased.

MATERIALS

9 (11, 13, 13, 14, 16, 17, 18, 19) skeins of Ocean by the Sea "Thicc" (100% merino wool; 76 yards/ 100 grams) in Wura Patina or approximately 685 (784, 865, 965, 1,050, 1,150, 1,250, 1,330, 1,430) yards of chunky-weight yarn

40" [100 cm] circular needles size US 11 [8 mm]

16" [40.5 cm] circular needles size US 10 [6 mm] and US 11 [8 mm]

Double pointed needles size US 10 [6 mm] and US 11 [8 mm]

Crochet hook size US K-10½ [6.5 mm]

Stitch markers

Scrap yarn

Point protectors

Tapestry needle

GAUGE

11 stitches and 15 rows = 4" [10 cm] over Stockinette Stitch using US 11 [8 mm] needles after blocking or size needed to obtain gauge

FINISHED MEASUREMENTS

This piece is designed to be form fitting with 2–4" [5–10 cm] of ease. Sample shown in size 44¼ [112 cm].

Chest: 36¼ (40, 44¼, 48, 52¼, 56, 60¼, 64, 68¼)" [92 (101.5, 112.5, 122, 132.5, 142, 153, 162.5, 173) cm]

Length to underarm: 16½" [42 cm]

Circumference at underarm: 11 (11½, 12½, 13¾, 14½, 16, 17½, 18, 19)" [28 (29, 31.5, 35, 37, 40.5, 44.5, 45.5, 48) cm]

Sleeve length: 18½" [47 cm]

Next Row: k3, sl1yo, purl to last 4 stitches, sl1yo, slip 3 purlwise wyif.

Repeat Increase Row and following WS row twice more—100 (110, 122, 132, 144, 154, 166, 176, 188) stitches.

Next Row (RS): k3, BRK, LLI, k2tog, knit to last 7 stitches, skp, RLI, BRK, slip 3 purlwise wyif.

Next Row: k3, sl1yo, purl to last 4 stitches, sl1yo, slip 3 purlwise wyif.

Repeat last 2 rows until piece measures 5½" [14 cm] from bottom of I-Cord edge, ending with WS row.

WAIST SHAPING

Note: Read through this section before you continue to knit. Waist Shaping and Built-In Pockets are worked at the same time.

Decrease Row (RS): k3, BRK, LLI, k2tog, knit to marker, slm, k4, skp, knit to 6 stitches before next marker, k2tog, k4, slm, knit to last 7 stitches, skp, RLI, BRK, slip 3 purlwise wyif—2 stitches decreased.

Repeat Decrease Row every 4th row 4 more times—90 (100, 112, 122, 134, 144, 156, 166, 178) stitches.

Work even for 3 rows.

Increase Row (RS): k3, BRK, LLI, k2tog, knit to marker, slm, k4, LLI, knit to 5 stitches before next marker, RLI, k4, slm, knit to last 7 stitches, skp, RLI, BRK, slip 3 purlwise wyif—2 stitches increased.

Repeat Increase Row every 4th row 4 more times—100 (110, 122, 132, 144, 154, 166, 176, 188) stitches.

AT THE SAME TIME work Built-In Pockets when 20 rows have been worked from beginning of pockets and piece measures approximately 7½" [19 cm] from bottom of I-Cord edge, ending with a WS row. Leave body stitches on hold on working needle while you make and attach the Built-In Pockets.

BUILT-IN POCKETS

Note: Pocket rows are joined to the body each row. The outer edge is left open for the pocket opening.

Right Front Pocket

Slip 15 (15, 15, 15, 17, 17, 19, 19, 21) pocket stitches purlwise to US 11 [8 mm] dpn.

Row 1: with RS facing, join a new ball of yarn and knit 1 row.

Row 2: purl to last pocket stitch, slip 1 purlwise wyif; on the main body of work and with LH needle, pick up a row ladder on the main body to the left of the stitch directly behind the last stitch you just slipped; move the slipped stitch purlwise wyif back to the LH needle and p2tog.

Row 3: pick up the next row ladder up to the right of the first stitch on the pocket and place on the LH needle, k2tog, knit to end.

Repeat Rows 2 and 3 for 8 more times, then repeat Row 2 once more, so that the pocket stitches are parallel to the stitches on the 40" [60 cm] circular. Place point protectors on each side of your dpns to secure the live pocket stitches while you make and attach the Left Front Pocket.

Left Front Pocket

Slip 15 (15, 15, 15, 17, 17, 19, 19, 21) pocket stitches purlwise to US 11 [8 mm] dpn.

Row 1: with RS facing, join a new ball of yarn and knit 1 row.

Row 2: slip the first stitch off the needle knitwise, then slip it back to the LH needle purlwise, wyib pick up a row ladder on the main body to the right of the stitch directly behind the stitch you just turned and place on LH needle, p2tog tbl, purl to end.

Row 3: knit to last stitch, slip 1 knitwise wyib, pick up next row ladder up on the main body to the left of the last stitch on the pocket and place on the RH needle, k2tog tbl.

Repeat from * to * as for Right Front Pocket.

Note: Use a dpn to neaten up the joining knit stitch on the RS of work and distribute looseness into neighboring stitches.

JOIN TOP POCKET SEAMS TO BODY

Return to Body stitches on working needle and join pockets as follows:

Next Row (RS): k3, BRK, LLI, k2tog, k2, *[insert needle into next stitch on pocket then into next stitch on body and knit 2 stitches together] 15 (15, 15, 15, 17, 17, 19, 19, 21) times*, work as established to last marker, k1 (4, 7, 9, 10, 13, 14, 16, 17), repeat from * to *, k2, skp, RLI, BRK, slip 3 purlwise wyif.

Continue Waist Shaping as established, then work even until piece measures 16½" [42 cm] from below I-Cord edge, ending with a RS row.

ESTABLISH UNDERARMS

Next Row (WS): k3, sl1yo, [purl to 2 (2, 3, 3, 3, 4, 5, 6, 6) stitches after next marker, slip last 4 (4, 6, 6, 6, 8, 10, 12, 12) stitches onto a stitch holder or scrap yarn, removing marker] 2 times, purl to last 4 stitches, sl1yo, slip 3 purlwise wyif—23 (26, 28, 30, 33, 35, 37, 38, 41) stitches for each Front and 46 (50, 54, 60, 66, 68, 72, 76, 82) stitches for Back; 92 (102, 110, 120, 132, 138, 146, 152, 164) stitches total.

Do not break yarn; set Body aside and make Sleeves.

sleeves

Work Knit Hem as follows: using Crochet Chain Provisional Cast On, crochet hook and scrap yarn, chain 26 (26, 26, 28, 28, 28, 30, 30, 32) stitches. Cut 4" [10 cm] of tail and fasten off. With US 10 [6 mm] dpns, pick up and knit 24 (24, 24, 26, 26, 26, 28, 28, 30) into the back loop of each crochet chain. Evenly divide stitches onto three US 10 [6 mm] dpns, place marker, and join for working in the round.

Work even in Stockinette Stitch, knitting every round for 42 rounds.

JOIN SLEEVE CUFF

Place point protectors on dpns as needed to secure sleeve stitches. Remove scrap yarn from provisional cast on edge and place live stitches onto 16" [40.5 cm] circular needles size US 10 [6 mm]. Fold sleeve cuff in half to WS so purl sides are facing each other. With working dpn and working yarn, *insert needle into next stitch on front needle then into next stitch on 16" [40 cm] circular needles and knit 2 stitches together*; repeat from * to * until all stitches are joined.

Change to US 11 [8 mm] dpns.

Next Round: Knit.

Work even for 9 (9, 9, 9, 5, 5, 5, 1, 1) more rounds.

Increase Round: k2, RLI, knit to last 3 stitches, LLI, k2—2 stitches increased.

Repeat Increase Round every 10 (8, 8, 6, 6, 4, 4, 4, 4) rounds 2 (3, 4, 5, 6, 8, 9, 10, 10) more times—30 (32, 34, 38, 40, 44, 48, 50, 52) stitches.

Note: Change to 16" [40.5 cm] circular needles size US 11 [8 mm] when necessary.

Work even in Stockinette Stitch until piece measures 18½" [47 cm] from edge of Sleeve Cuff.

ESTABLISH UNDERARMS

Next Round: knit to last 2 (2, 3, 3, 3, 4, 5, 6, 6) stitches, slip next 4 (4, 6, 6, 6, 8, 10, 12, 12) stitches onto stitch holder or scrap yarn, removing marker. Slip remaining 26 (28, 28, 32, 34, 36, 38, 38, 40) stitches onto 16" [40.5 cm] circular needles size US 10 [6 mm].

Make one more identical Sleeve, leaving remaining stitches of second Sleeve on 16" [40.5 cm] circular needles size 11 [8 mm].

yoke

JOIN SLEEVES TO BODY AND BEGIN SHAPING COLLAR

Joining Row (RS): With RS of Body facing and using working yarn attached to Body, k3, BRK, LLI, knit across Right Front stitches, *pm, k26 (28, 28, 32, 34, 36, 38, 38, 40) Sleeve stitches, pm,* k46 (50, 54, 60, 66, 68, 72, 76, 82) Back stitches, repeat from * to * for second Sleeve, knit to last 5 stitches of Left Front, RLI, BRK, slip 3 purlwise wyif—2 stitches increased; 146 (160, 168, 186, 202, 212, 224, 230, 246) stitches total.

Next Row (WS): k3, sl1yo, purl to last 4 stitches, sl1yo, slip 3 purlwise wyif.

SHAPE RAGLANS

For sizes - (-, 44¼, 48, 52¼, 56, 60¼, 64, 68¼)″ [- (-, 112.5, 122, 132.5, 142, 153, 162.5, 173) cm] only

Raglan Decrease Row 1 (RS): k3, BRK, LLI, [knit to 4 stitches before next marker, k3tog, k2, slm, k2, skp, knit to 4 stitches before next marker, k2tog, k2, slm, k2, sk2p] twice, knit to last 5 stitches, RLI, BRK, slip 3 purlwise wyif—12 stitches decreased at raglans; 2 stitches increased at front edges.

Repeat Raglan Decrease Row 1 every RS row - (-, 1, 2, 4, 5, 6, 8, 10) more times—- (-, 27, 28, 29, 30, 31, 30, 31) stitches for each Front; - (-, 46, 48, 46, 44, 44, 40, 38) stitches for Back; - (-, 24, 26, 24, 24, 24, 20, 18) stitches for each Sleeve; - (-, 148, 156, 152, 152, 154, 140, 136) stitches total.

Work 1 WS row even.

For all sizes

Raglan Decrease Row 2 (RS): k3, BRK, LLI, [knit to 4 stitches before next marker, k2tog, k2, slm, k2, skp, knit to 4 stitches before next marker, k2tog, k2, slm, k2, skp] twice, knit to last 5 stitches, RLI, BRK, slip 3 purlwise wyif—8 stitches decreased at raglans; 2 stitches increased at front edges.

Repeat Raglan Decrease Row 2 every RS row 9 (10, 8, 9, 8, 8, 8, 6, 5) more times— 24 (27, 27, 28, 29, 30, 31, 30, 31) stitches for each Front; 26 (28, 28, 28, 28, 26, 26, 26, 26) stitches for Back; 6 stitches for each Sleeve; 86 (94, 94, 96, 98, 98, 100, 98, 100) stitches total.

Work 1 WS row even.

CONTINUE SHAPING RAGLAN

Decrease Row 1 (RS): k3, BRK, LLI, knit to 4 stitches before next marker, k2tog, k2, slm, k2, k2tog, k2, slm, k2, skp, knit to 4 stitches before next marker, k2tog, k2, slm, k2, skp, k2, slm, k2, skp, knit to last 5 stitches, RLI, BRK, slip 3 purlwise wyif—24 (27, 27, 28, 29, 30, 31, 30, 31) stitches for each Front; 24 (26, 26, 26, 26, 24, 24, 24, 24) stitches for Back; 5 stitches for each Sleeve; 82 (90, 90, 92, 94, 94, 96, 94, 96) stitches total.

Work 1 WS row even.

Decrease Row 2: k3, BRK, LLI, knit to 4 stitches before next marker, k2tog, k2, slm, k1, k2tog, k2, slm, k2, skp, knit to 4 stitches before next marker, k2tog, k2, sm, k2, skp, k1, slm, k2, skp, knit to last 5 stitches, RLI, BRK, slip 3 purlwise wyif—24 (27, 27, 28, 29, 30, 31, 30, 31) stitches for each Front; 22 (24, 24, 24, 24, 22, 22, 22, 22) stitches for Back; 4 stitches for each Sleeve; 78 (86, 86, 88, 90, 90, 92, 90, 92) stitches total.

Work 1 WS row even.

Decrease Row 3: k3, BRK, LLI, knit to 4 stitches before next marker, k2tog, k2, remove marker, k2tog, k2, slm, k2, skp, knit to 4 stitches before next marker, k2tog, k2, sm, k2, skp, remove marker, k2, skp, knit to last 5 stitches, RLI, BRK, slip 3 purlwise wyif—27 (30, 30, 31, 32, 33, 34, 33, 34) stitches for each Front; 20 (22, 22, 22, 22, 20, 20, 20, 20) stitches for Back; 74 (82, 82, 84, 86, 86, 88, 86, 88) stitches total.

Work 1 WS row even.

Decrease Row 4: k3, BRK, LLI, knit to 7 stitches before next marker, k2tog, k1, k2tog, k2, slm, k2, skp, knit to 4 stitches before next marker, k2tog, k2, slm, k2, skp, k1, skp, knit to last 5 stitches, RLI, BRK, slip 3 purlwise wyif—26 (29, 29, 30, 31, 32, 33, 32, 33) stitches for each Front; 18 (20, 20, 20, 20, 18, 18, 18, 18) stitches for Back; 70 (78, 78, 80, 82, 82, 84, 82, 84) stitches total.

Work 1 WS row even.

Note: For size 36¼" [92 cm] only, skip Decrease Row 5 and following row; go to Decrease Row 6.

Decrease Row 5: k3, BRK, LLI, knit to 6 stitches before next marker, [k2tog] 2 times, k2, slm, k2, skp, knit to 4 stitches before next marker, k2tog, k2, slm, k2, [skp] 2 times, knit to last 5 stitches, RLI, BRK, slip 3 purlwise wyif—- (28, 28, 29, 30, 31, 32, 31, 32) stitches for each Front; - (18, 18, 18, 18, 16, 16, 16, 16) stitches for Back; - (74, 74, 76, 78, 78, 80, 78, 80) stitches total.

Work 1 WS row even.

CONTINUE SHAPING RAGLAN

Decrease Row 6: k3, BRK, LLI, knit to 4 stitches before next marker, k2tog, k2, slm, k2, skp, knit to 4 stitches before next marker, k2tog, k2, slm, k2, skp, knit to last 5 stitches, RLI, BRK, slip 3 purlwise wyif—26 (28, 28, 29, 30, 31, 32, 31, 32) stitches for each Front; 16 (16, 16, 16, 16, 14, 14, 14, 14) stitches for Back; 68 (72, 72, 74, 76, 76, 78, 76, 78) stitches total.

Work 1 WS row even.

Repeat last 2 rows 0 (2, 2, 2, 2, 2, 2, 2, 2) more times—26 (28, 28, 29, 30, 31, 32, 31, 32) stitches for each Front; 16 (12, 12, 12, 12, 10, 10, 10, 10) stitches for Back; 68 (68, 68, 70, 72, 72, 74, 72, 74) stitches total.

collar

JOIN RIGHT FRONT COLLAR TO BACK NECK

Joining Short Row (RS): k3, BRK, LLI, k2tog, k18 (18, 18, 19, 20, 20, 21, 20, 21), skp, turn to the WS, slip 1 purlwise wyif, purl to last 4 stitches, sl1yo, slip 3 purlwise wyif.

Repeat Joining Short Row 6 more times, removing marker on last row.

CONTINUE SHAPING COLLAR WITH WRAP & TURN SHORT ROWS

Short Row 1 (RS): k3, BRK, LLI, k2tog, k16, W&T, purl to last 4 stitches, sl1yo, slip 3 purlwise wyif.

Short Row 2: k3, BRK, LLI, k2tog, knit to 2 stitches before next wrap, W&T, purl to last 4 stitches, sl1yo, slip 3 purlwise wyif.

Repeat Short Row 2 for 6 more times.

Next Short Row (RS): k2, BRK, LLI, k2tog, W&T, p3, sl1yo, slip 3 purlwise wyif.

Pick Up Short Rows (WS): k3, BRK, LLI, k2tog, [pick up wrap, k1] 9 times, skp, knit to marker, remove marker, knit to last 7 stitches, skp, RLI, BRK, slip 3 purlwise wyif.

JOIN LEFT SIDE OF COLLAR TO BACK NECK

Joining Short Row (WS): k3, sl1yo, p21 (21, 21, 22, 23, 23, 24, 23, 24), p2tog, turn to RS, slip 1 purlwise wyib, knit to last 7 stitches, skp, RLI, BRK, slip 3 purlwise wyif.

Repeat Joining Short Row 6 more times.

CONTINUE SHAPING COLLAR

Short Row 1 (WS): k3, sl1yo, p19, W&T, knit to last 7 stitches, skp, RLI, BRK, slip 3 purlwise wyif.

Short Row 2: k3, sl1yo, purl to 2 stitches before next wrap, W&T, knit to last 7 stitches, skp, RLI, BRK, slip 3 purlwise wyif.

Repeat Short Row 2 for 6 more times.

Next Short Row (WS): k3, sl1yo, p3, W&T, skp, RLI, BRK, slip 3 purlwise wyif.

Pick Up Short Rows (WS): k3, p4, [pick up wrap, p1] 9 times, p2tog—52 (52, 52, 54, 56, 56, 58, 56, 58) stitches; 26 (26, 26, 27, 28, 28, 29, 28, 29) stitches for each half of Collar.

finishing

SEAM COLLAR

Fold Collar in half so purl sides are facing each other. Join seam using Kitchener Stitch to last 3 stitches on each needle, slip last 3 stitches on Left Side of Collar onto a dpn and twist needle so the knit side of stitches is facing you before joining I-Cord edges.

KNIT HEM BIND OFF ON POCKETS

With US 10 [6 mm] dpns and RS facing, pick up and knit 17 stitches evenly spaced along pocket opening. Work 4 rows of Stockinette Stitch, beginning with a purl row.

Joining Row (WS): Fold hem in half to WS so knit side is facing, insert tapestry needle into the first purl bump in first row below, insert tapestry needle knitwise into first stitch on needle and drop off the needle, pull taut. *Insert tapestry needle into the next purl bump in first row below, insert tapestry needle knitwise into next stitch on needle and drop off the needle, pull taut; repeat from * until all stitches are joined to inside of pocket. Join edges of pocket trim to main body using Seaming Bind Off to Selvedge. Join the pocket trim to just 1 stitch on the main body. You'll have to pick up 2 to 3 horizontal ladders next to the selvedge edge on the pocket trim to one half of the knit stitch on body. If it does not look good to you the first time, take it out and try again. That's what I had to do! It takes some fudging and will come together beautifully.

SEAM UNDERARMS

Slip corresponding Sleeve and Body stitches on hold at Underarm onto separate US 11 [8 mm] dpns and hold parallel with WS together. Seam stitches using Kitchener Stitch.

WASH AND BLOCK

Weave in all ends. Soak the cardigan in cool water using a gentle woolen soap for 10 to 15 minutes. Reshape to final measurements and lay flat to dry. Steam block to improve the overall finish at the bottom edge and around the pockets.

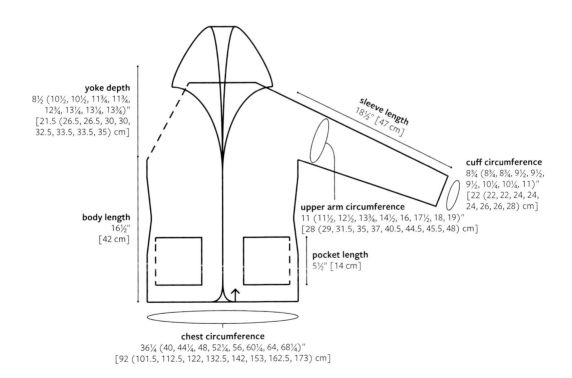

yoke depth
8½ (10½, 10½, 11¾, 11¾, 12¾, 13¼, 13¼, 13¾)"
[21.5 (26.5, 26.5, 30, 30, 32.5, 33.5, 33.5, 35) cm]

sleeve length
18½" [47 cm]

cuff circumference
8¾ (8¾, 8¾, 9½, 9½, 9½, 10¼, 10¼, 11)"
[22 (22, 22, 24, 24, 24, 26, 26, 28) cm]

body length
16½"
[42 cm]

upper arm circumference
11 (11½, 12½, 13¾, 14½, 16, 17½, 18, 19)"
[28 (29, 31.5, 35, 37, 40.5, 44.5, 45.5, 48) cm]

pocket length
5½" [14 cm]

chest circumference
36¼ (40, 44¼, 48, 52¼, 56, 60¼, 64, 68¼)"
[92 (101.5, 112.5, 122, 132.5, 142, 153, 162.5, 173) cm]

audre

aw-dree

---

noun

noble strength

"TO SEARCH FOR POWER WITHIN MYSELF MEANS I MUST BE WILLING TO MOVE THROUGH BEING AFRAID TO WHATEVER LIES BEYOND. IF I LOOK AT MY MOST VULNERABLE PLACES AND ACKNOWLEDGE THE PAIN I HAVE FELT, I CAN REMOVE THE SOURCE OF THAT PAIN FROM MY ENEMIES' ARSENALS. MY HISTORY CANNOT BE USED TO FEATHER MY ENEMIES' ARROWS THEN, AND THAT LESSENS THEIR POWER OVER ME. NOTHING I ACCEPT ABOUT MYSELF CAN BE USED AGAINST ME TO DIMINISH ME. I AM WHO I AM, DOING WHAT I CAME TO DO, ACTING UPON YOU LIKE A DRUG OR A CHISEL TO REMIND YOU OF YOUR ME-NESS, AS I DISCOVER YOU IN MYSELF."

—Audre Lorde

Audre Lorde is an armored suit, soft and malleable. Her words protect me from myself, drawing attention to the gap between living fully in my potential and hiding from visibility. I'm in this weird place of wanting to lead and support my communities abundantly, but not wanting anyone to actually see me. Of wanting to show up vulnerably, but still uneasy about how those who bear witness to my story will digest it. I wonder what Lorde would discover about herself through me. I know from the intentions she set forth in her books that I am one of the people—Black, woman, and falling in love with dark women— her work is designed for. I acknowledge that I do not yet have it all figured out. I have a long way to go and many lessons to explore.

How small can I become so no one notices me at all?

How far can I run in the other direction of my fear before my goals become a faint mirage?

How long can I deny my purpose before I feel like it never really mattered at all?

I've waited for many years to catch up with myself. I've spent so much time running in the opposite direction, doing what I thought I should be doing. I see myself in these pages trying to find the words to describe what it looks like to heal our shrunken parts. To show you what the path can look like to be courageous while still feeling fear. To remind you of just how powerful you are with the help of our ancestors and peers. To remind you: you are not alone. The road is not linear. It's messy and humbling. We have a squad of revolutionary women who, like me, write to save us from the systems that would keep us glued to the idea that it is too late, too hard, too expensive to be in control of our own destiny.

In Lorde's collection *A Burst of Light*, several times she says, "I have done good work." Even the most prolific among us need to write reassuring love letters to ourselves.

I have done good work.

I have done good work.

I have done good work.

Your life, your story, your words have meaning. You have done good work.

Making the Audre Cowl will help you exercise being regal and proud. It will test the dexterity of your hands. Your stitches will feel snug on the needle. Knit with ease, erring on the looser side. We will make two crochet seams to define what I like to call the spine. Bringing an extra-bulky yarn down two needle sizes creates a much denser fabric. This helps to stiffen the collar. The snug feeling will become easier as you go along. When decreasing the crochet seam stitch, you'll need to knit on the tips of your needles. I recommend working crochet seams in separate sessions if you find yourself tensing up. Put it down and come back once you charge up. Even after washing and blocking, Audre's collar can stand up on its own. Wear it and put yourself on a pedestal.

audre cowl

shoulder

Using US 13 [9 mm] needles, CO 55 (63, 71, 79, 87, 93, 101) stitches using Tubular Cast On.

Foundation Row 1: *k1tbl, slip 1 purlwise wyif; repeat from * to last stitch, end k1.

Foundation Row 2: slip 1 knitwise wyib, *k1, slip 1 purlwise wyif; repeat from * to last 2 stitches, k2. Do not turn.

Joining round: pm to mark beginning of round, k1 to join round, being careful not to twist stitches, *k1, p1; repeat from * to last 2 stitches, k2.

SHAPE SHOULDER

Change to US 17 [12 mm] needle.

Next Round: k1, purl to last stitch, k1.

Rounds 1 and 3: knit.

Round 2: k1, purl to last stitch, k1.

Decrease Round 4: k1, p7 (11, 11, 11, 15, 17, 17), [p2tog, p9 (10, 12, 14, 15, 16, 18)] 4 times, p2tog, k1—5 stitches decreased; 50 (58, 66, 74, 82, 88, 96) stitches total.

Rounds 5–7: Repeat Rounds 1–3.

Decrease Round 8: k1, p6 (10, 10, 10, 14, 16, 16), [p2tog, p8 (9, 11, 13, 14, 15, 17)] 4 times, p2tog, k1—5 stitches decreased; 45 (53, 61, 69, 77, 83, 91) stitches total.

Rounds 9–11: Repeat Rounds 1–3.

Decrease Round 12: k1, p5 (9, 9, 9, 13, 15, 15), p2tog, p7 (8, 10, 12, 13, 14, 16), p2tog, p5 (4, 6, 8, 7, 7, 9), k1 (center stitch), p1 (3, 3, 3, 5, 6, 6), [p2tog, p7 (8, 10, 12, 13, 14, 16)] twice, p2, k1—4 stitches decreased; 41 (49, 57, 65, 73, 79, 87) stitches total.

MATERIALS

5 skein Purl Soho "Gentle Giant" (100% merino wool; 48 yards/ 125 grams) in Winter Bark or approximately 240 yards [220 m] of extra-bulky-weight yarn

24" [60 cm] circular needles size US 13 [9 mm] and US 17 [12 mm]

Crochet hook size US G [4.25 mm]

Stitch markers

Removable stitch marker or scrap yarn

Tapestry needle

Scissors

GAUGE

6 stitches and 15 rounds = 4" [10 cm] over Garter Stitch using US 17 [12 mm] needles or size to obtain gauge

FINISHED MEASUREMENTS

This piece is designed to have a natural fit over the shoulders with 2–3" [5–7.5 cm] of ease. Shown in size 47¼" [120 cm] with 2–3" [5–7.5 cm] of ease over shoulder.

Circumference at shoulder edge: 36½ (42, 47¼, 52½, 58, 62, 67¼)" [92.5 (106.5, 120, 133, 147, 157.5, 170.5) cm]

Neck circumference at smallest point: 28" [71 cm]

Length at center back: 15¼ (16¾, 18, 19, 20, 21¼, 21¾)" [38.5 (42.5, 45.5, 48, 51, 54, 55) cm]

separate at center front

Note: The next round is worked to the center stitch, then the cowl is turned to work back and forth in rows. The beginning-of-round marker will now be at the center of the row. Continue to slip this marker.

Foundation Row: k15 (19, 23, 27, 31, 34, 38), skp, p3, slip center stitch to removable stitch marker to secure, turn to work back and forth in rows, k19 (23, 27, 31, 35, 38, 42), slip beginning-of-round marker (now center row marker), p15 (19, 23, 27, 31, 34, 38), p2tog, k3—2 stitches decreased; 1 stitch placed on marker; 38 (46, 54, 62, 70, 76, 84) stitches on needles.

decrease section 1

Row 1 (RS): purl to 1 stitch before center marker, k1, slm, knit to last 5 stitches, skp, p3—1 stitch decreased.

Row 2: knit to 1 stitch before marker, p1, slm, purl to last 5 stitches, p2tog, k3—1 stitch decreased.

Repeat Rows 1 and 2 of Decrease Section 1 for 4 (6, 6, 6, 6, 7, 5) more times—28 (32, 40, 48, 56, 60, 72) stitches.

decrease section 2

Change to US 13 [8 mm] needles.

Row 1 (RS): p3, p2tog, purl to 1 stitch before marker, k1, slm, knit to last 5 stitches, skp, p3—2 stitches decreased.

Row 2: k3, skp, knit to 1 stitch before marker, p1, slm, purl to last 5 stitches, p2tog, k3—2 stitches decreased.

Repeat Rows 1 and 2 of Decrease Section 2 for 3 (4, 6, 8, 10, 11, 14) more times—12 stitches.

make crochet seams

Next Row (RS): p5, *turn to WS, using crochet hook, create a crochet seam (see page 58) between the needles beginning just above the Tubular Cast On, place seam stitch onto the RH needle purlwise and turn to RS of work*, with working yarn, k2tog (knit next stitch together with seam stitch), slip 1 knitwise, repeat from * to * once, with working yarn, k1 seam stitch, psso, p5.

shape rib collar

Foundation Round: Pick up and knit 32 stitches along neck edge to center stitch, k1 (center stitch) from removable stitch marker, pick up and knit 32 stitches along selvedge edge, then working across first 6 back neck stitches, [k1, p1] 3 times—77 stitches.

Pm to mark new beginning of round.

Round 1: p1, byo, [k1, p1] 18 times, s2kp, [p1, k1] 18 times, yo, p1.

Round 2: p1, p1tfl (purl 1 through front loop, knit the knits and purl the purls to last 2 stitches, p1tbl, p1.

Round 3: p2, byo, [k1, p1] 17 times, k1, s2kp, k1, [p1, k1] 17 times, yo, p2.

Round 4 and following even rounds: knit the knits and purl the purls, closing byo and yo eyelets as established.

Round 5: p3, byo, [k1, p1] 17 times, s2kp, [p1, k1] 17 times, yo, p3.

Round 7: p4, byo, [k1, p1] 16 times, k1, s2kp, k1, [p1, k1] 16 times, yo, p4.

Round 9: p5, byo, [k1, p1] 16 times, s2kp, [p1, k1] 16 times, yo, p5.

Round 11: p6, byo, [k1, p1] 15 times, k1, s2kp, k1, [p1, k1] 15 times, yo, p6.

Round 13: p7, byo, [k1, p1] 15 times, s2kp, [p1, k1] 15 times, yo, p7.

Round 15: p8, byo, [k1, p1] 14 times, k1, s2kp, k1, [p1, k1] 14 times, p8—1 stitch decreased; 76 stitches total.

Round 17: p9, [k1, p1] 14 times, s2kp, [p1, k1] 14 times, p8—2 stitches decreased; 74 stitches total.

Round 18: [p1, k1] to 3 center front stitches, s2kp, [k1, p1] repeat to last stitch, k1—2 stitches decreased; 72 stitches total.

Round 19: [p1, k1] 17 times, p1, s2kp, [p1, k1] 17 times—2 stitches decreased; 70 stitches total.

Work Crochet Bind Off, knitting the knits and purling the purls.

finishing

Weave in all ends. Soak the cowl in cool water using a gentle woolen soap for 10 to 15 minutes. Reshape and lay flat to dry.

sola

sow·laa

---

adverb or adjective

feminine form of *solus*; alone or unaccompanied
(used especially as a stage direction)

"SOLITUDE CAN BE A MUCH-TO-BE-DESIRED CONDITION. NOT ONLY IS IT ACCEPTABLE TO BE ALONE, AT TIMES IT IS POSITIVELY TO BE WISHED FOR. IT IS IN THE INTERLUDES BETWEEN BEING IN COMPANY THAT WE TALK TO OURSELVES. IN THE SILENCE WE LISTEN TO OURSELVES. THEN WE ASK QUESTIONS OF OURSELVES. WE DESCRIBE OURSELVES, AND IN THE QUIETUDE, WE MAY EVEN HEAR THE VOICE OF GOD."

—Maya Angelou

Pack the knitting and go away for a short time. Take yourself out on a date. A walk. Drive a car. Fly a plane. I am a big fan of long bus rides across state lines and seeing the miraculous transformation of New York City skyscrapers and brownstones into widespread farmland surrounded by lonely* lakes.

For $8, the Metro-North travels along the Hudson River to Upstate New York. October is for peeping leaves. For waterfront views, I sit on the left side of the train. Snacks packed and half eaten, I hop off ninety minutes from home.

Visit a nearby park and find a quiet bench. Break out the podcast, let the rustling of leaves guide your breathing, stretch out on a picnic blanket. Knit. Choose what feels right in the moment. Maybe for thirty minutes. Maybe for a day. Blessed be a week.

Do one. Do all.

Just do not forget your knitting. And don't forget your snacks.

Sola can be made over a weekend. One long stretch of relaxation for dramatic effect.

---

* I use and explore many words that describe time lived without company, and it is very rare that the word describes sad or unpleasant experiences. This "lonely" lake is happy.

sola scarf

Work I-Cord Cast On as follows: Using Crochet Chain Provisional Cast On, crochet hook, and scrap yarn, chain 5 stitches. Cut 4" [10 cm] of tail and fasten off.

Using US 15 [10 mm] dpns, pick up and knit 3 stitches into the back loops of the crochet chain. Work I-Cord for 22 rows. Slip the 3 stitches onto 24" [60 cm] circular needles size US 17 [12 mm], pick up and knit 20 stitches into the top half of the first stitch of each row along the I-Cord. Carefully remove the scrap yarn from the provisional cast on, slipping 3 live stitches onto the RH needle with the purl side facing you and the working yarn in front—26 stitches.

Foundation Row (WS): k6, sl1yo, k12, sl1yo, k3, slip 3 purlwise wyif.

Row 1 (RS): k5, sl1yo, BRK, k12, BRK, sl1yo, k2, slip 3 purlwise wyif.

Row 2: k5, BRK, sl1yo, k12, sl1yo, BRK, k2, slip 3 purlwise wyif.

Repeat last 2 rows until there are 105 Garter ridges, ending with Row 2.

Next Row (RS): k5, p1, BRK, k12, BRK, p1, k2, slip 3 purlwise wyif.

i-cord bind off

Work I-Cord Bind Off as follows: *k2, skp, slip 3 stitches from RH needle back to LH needle; repeat from * until 6 stitches remain. Using Kitchener Stitch, seam I-Cord stitches together.

finishing

Weave in all ends. Soak the scarf in cool water using a gentle woolen soap for 10 to 15 minutes. Reshape and lay flat to dry.

MATERIALS

7 skeins Purl Soho "Gentle Giant" (100% merino wool; 48 yards/ 125 grams) in Silver Mauve or approximately 336 yards [307 m] of bulky-weight yarn

24" [60 cm] circular needles size US 17 [12 mm]

Double pointed needles size US 15 [10 mm]

Crochet hook size US N/P-15 [10 mm]

Scrap yarn

Tapestry needle

Scissors

GAUGE

6 stitches and 10 rows = 4" [10 cm] over Garter Stitch using US 17 [12 mm] needles or size needed to obtain gauge

FINISHED MEASUREMENTS

Length: 70" [177.5 cm]
Width: 14" [35.5 cm]

aura

aw·ruh

---

noun

an emanation surrounding the body of a living
creature and regarded as an essential part of the
individual, as from a gentle breeze

"I AM MY OWN. I AM ENOUGH. I AM ROOTED IN LOVE. MY LIFE IS ABUNDANT. MY HEART IS RESILIENT. MY HAPPINESS IS IMPORTANT. NOTHING HAS THE POWER TO BREAK OR DESTROY ME. I AM WHOLE EVEN THROUGH HURT."

—Alex Elle

You are an alchemist.

You are the seed.

The sun.

And the water.

A bright ring of light.

The Aura Cowl is a ring you can knit in one sitting to elevate your whole vibe in a breeze.

aura cowl

Using the Crochet Chain Provisional Cast On, crochet hook, and scrap yarn, chain 23 stitches. Cut 4" [10 cm] of tail and fasten off. Using US 15 [10 mm] circular needles, pick up and knit 21 stitches into the back loops of the crochet chain.

Change to US 17 [12 mm] needles.

Foundation Row (WS): k3, [sl1yo, k1] 8 times, k2.

Row 1 (RS): slip 1 knitwise wyib, k1, [sl1yo, BRK] 8 times, sl1yo, k2.

Row 2: slip 1 knitwise wyib, k1, [BRK, sl1yo] 8 times, BRK, k2.

Repeat last 2 rows until piece measures approximately 24" [60 cm] from cast on edge, ending with a Row 2.

Next Row (RS): slip 1 knitwise wyib, k1, [p1, BRK] 8 times, p1, k2.

Carefully remove the scrap yarn from the provisional cast on, slipping 21 live stitches onto the US 15 [10 mm] needle. With working yarn and RS facing each other, join edges together using the 3-Needle Bind Off.

finishing

Weave in all ends. Soak the cowl in cool water using a gentle woolen soap for 10 to 15 minutes. Reshape and lay flat to dry.

MATERIALS

3 skeins Purl Soho "Gentle Giant" (100% merino wool; 48 yards/ 125 grams) in Elephant Gray, or approximately 120 yards [110 m] of bulky-weight yarn

16" [40.5 cm] circular needles size US 15 [10 mm]

24" [60 cm] circular needles size US 17 [12 mm]

Crochet hook size US N/P-15 [10 mm]

Scrap yarn

Tapestry needle

Scissors

GAUGE

6 stitches and 10 rows = 4" [10 cm] over Brioche Stitch using US 17 [12 mm] needles or size needed to obtain gauge

FINAL MEASUREMENTS

Circumference: 26" [66 cm]

Width: 14" [38.5 cm]

terran

teh·ruhn

---

noun

an inhabitant of the planet Earth

"SELF-DEFINITION AND SELF-DETERMINATION IS ABOUT
THE MANY VARIED DECISIONS THAT WE MAKE TO
COMPOSE AND JOURNEY TOWARD OURSELVES, ABOUT
THE AUDACITY AND STRENGTH TO PROCLAIM, CREATE,
AND EVOLVE INTO WHO WE KNOW OURSELVES TO BE."

—Janet Mock

Over the summer of 2020, I gathered virtually with a community of
women, nonbinary, and trans strategists of color—for a strategy for Black lives
workshop series hosted by Vanessa Newman and Kaylah Burton. The first
speaker, Sloan Leo, introduced me to community design—the application of
social justice values to design.

How do we nourish and define ourselves?
How do we translate our skills into impactful transformative justice campaigns?
How do we hold each other accountable in the work?
How do we support one another?
How do I actualize our vision for a liberated Black queer future?
How can we weave care into everything we make?

What is your ministry? What remedies do you have to offer a world in need of
deep healing? I like to think of the making landscape as a community garden
where every person is a part of a family of plants needing their own amount of
sun, water, tender care, and attention. We all have the nutrients needed to help
our neighbors thrive, whether we realize it or not. We are in a special season of
tending the gardens of Black people, Black history, Black art, and Black joy.

We are a powerful people experiencing a renaissance, journeying toward a
safer place for all of earth's inhabitants.

The Terran Hat features the Bloom Stitch, a combination of knits and purls,
different increases and decreases, twists and turns brought together into one
unified textured fabric. The most laborious and satisfying process is bringing
three stitches together as one and birthing three new stitches.

We will bloom together. Remember, when you rise, we all rise.

terran hat

Using US 10½ [6.5 mm] needles and Long Tail Cast On, CO 25 stitches.

Row 1 (RS): k3, p19, slip 3 purlwise wyif.

Row 2: k3, pm, [PYOP, k1] 4 times, PYOP, slip 3 purlwise wyif.

Row 3: knit to last 3 stitches, slm, slip 3 purlwise wyif.

Continue to slip marker.

Row 4: k3, p1, [k1, PYOP] 4 times, k1, p1, slip 3 purlwise wyif.

Row 5: Repeat Row 3.

shape hat

Increase Row 1 (WS): knit to marker, yo, slm, [PYOP, k1] 4 times, PYOP, slip 3 purlwise wyif—1 stitch increased.

Row 2 (RS): knit to marker, slm, p1tbl, purl to last 3 stitches, slip 3 purlwise wyif.

Row 3: knit to marker, slm, p1, [k1, PYOP] 4 times, k1, p1, slip 3 purlwise wyif.

Rows 4 and 6: knit to marker, slm, purl to last 3 stitches, slip 3 purlwise wyif.

Row 5: knit to marker, slm, [PYOP, k1] 4 times, PYOP, slip 3 purlwise wyif.

Row 7: knit to marker, slm, p1, [k1, PYOP] 4 times, k1, p1, slip 3 purlwise wyif.

Row 8: Repeat Row 4.

Repeat Increase Row 1 to Row 8 four more times—30 stitches.

Work 10 rows even in Bloom Stitch with I-Cord Selvedge and purling the purls on the RS as established.

MATERIALS

2 skeins Ocean by the Sea "Thicc" (100% merino wool; 76 yards/ 100 grams) in Ay Rosé or approximately 150 yards [140 m] of chunky-weight yarn

16" [40.5 cm] circular needles size US 10½ [6.5 mm]

Double pointed needles size US 9 [5.5 mm]

Crochet hook size US G-6 [4 mm]

Stitch markers

Tapestry needle

Scissors

GAUGE

13 stitches and 19 rows = 4" [10 cm] over Bloom Stitch using US 10½ [6.5 mm] needles or size to obtain gauge

FINISHED MEASUREMENTS

To fit 21–23" [53–58.5 cm] head circumference

Circumference along bottom edge: 23" [58 cm]

Length at center front: 9" [23 cm]

BLOOM STITCH

Multiple of 4 + 3 stitches

PYOP: purl 3 together, yarn over, purl same 3 stitches together

Rows 1 and 3 (RS): Knit.

Row 2: [PYOP, k1] to last 3 stitches, PYOP.

Row 4: p1, [k1, PYOP] to last 2 stitches, k1, p1

Decrease Row 1 (WS): knit to 2 stitches before marker, k2tog, slm, PYOP, k1] 4 times, PYOP, slip 3 purlwise wyif—1 stitch decreased.

Rows 2, 4, and 6: knit to marker, slm, purl to last 3 stitches, slip 3 purlwise wyif.

Rows 3 and 7: knit to marker, slm, p1, [k1, PYOP] 4 times, k1, p1, slip 3 purlwise wyif.

Row 5: knit to marker, slm, [PYOP, k1] 4 times, PYOP, slip 3 purlwise wyif.

Row 8: Repeat Row 2.

Repeat Decrease Row 1 to Row 8 three more times—26 stitches.

Work 7 rows even in Bloom Stitch with I-Cord Selvedge as established.

Last Decrease Row (RS): knit to 1 stitch before marker, slip 1, remove marker, k1, psso, slip 3 purlwise wyif—1 stitch decreased.

Next Row: k3, [PYOP, k1] 4 times, PYOP, slip 3 purlwise wyif.

Work 21 rows even in Bloom Stitch with I-Cord Selvedge as established.

BO knitwise using the Crochet Bind Off or Basic Knit Bind Off to last 3 stitches, slip last 3 stitches onto dpn, twist so knit side of I-Cord stitches are facing, BO remaining stitches knitwise and fasten off. Cut 24" [60 cm] of sewing tail.

seam body of hat

Lay hat flat with WS facing and shaping along bottom edge. Fold left side of hat over about 3" [7.5 cm] so the RS is facing. To create twist, bring bottom RH corner up to meet the top LH corner. Using Seaming Bind Off to bind off, join sides together.

crown

Using US 9 [5.5 mm] dpns and beginning at seam, pick up and knit 40 stitches on RS edge, then 8 stitches on WS edge, working into the first I-Cord stitch so 2 I-Cord stitches are facing on the RS—48 stitches.

Evenly divide the stitches onto 3 dpns, k1, pm to mark beginning of round.

Foundation Round: *k7, slip 1 purlwise wyib, pm; repeat from * around. For the last marker, pm of CC to mark beginning-of-round marker).

Decrease Round 1: *knit to 2 stitches before next marker, k2tog, slm; repeat from * around—6 stitches decreased.

Round 2: *knit to 1 stitch before next marker, slip 1 purlwise wyib, slm; repeat from * around.

Repeat last 2 rows 5 more times— 12 stitches.

Final Decrease Round: [k2tog] 6 times, removing all markers. Cut 8" [20 cm] of tail, weaving tail through remaining stitches to fasten off.

finishing

CRAB STITCH EDGING

Using the crochet hook, beginning at the bottom edge of the seam and working left to right, work Reverse Single Crochet, inserting hook into the purl stitches just above the seam.

WASH AND BLOCK

Weave in all ends. Soak the hat in cool water using a gentle woolen soap for 10 to 15 minutes. Reshape and lay flat to dry.

the land

Bless the land that welcomed us during all NYC seasons for several photo shoots to capture the outdoor images for this work. Your bird calls and tick warnings and dancing leaves were the country backdrop to our New York City light chase.

Shirley Chisholm State Park is on unceded land of the Lenape people, 407 acres large, a high-grass oasis surrounded by the Belt Parkway, Spring Creek Park, and Jamaica Bay, situated atop the former Pennsylvania Avenue and Fountain Avenue Landfills. An extensive stormwater management system was constructed to slow the flow of the stormwater down the hill and prevent erosion.

Chisholm was born in my hometown of Brooklyn on November 30, 1924. She was the first Black United States congresswoman and the first woman to run for the Democratic Party's presidential nomination. Her campaign slogan was "unbought and unbossed."

When asked about her legacy, she said, "I want to be remembered as a woman . . . who dared to be a catalyst of change."

photography

All images and self-portraits taken by the author—that's me—unless otherwise noted. Thank you, Storm Harper (photos on pages 2, 94, 97, and 98 created by Storm), Adrienne Colbert (photo on page 157 taken by Adrienne), and my handy-dandy camera remote and its two-second timer.

yarn and essentials

Ocean Rose botanically dyed the natural fibers and designed the color palette especially for this book. Thank you for your uplifting words, your intentional crafting of such magical experiences. You are an alchemist of the best kind. @ocean_bythesea

Special thank you to the team over at Purl Soho. Collaborating with you is always the highlight of my work. Your yarn is a daily delight and I'm always excited to see what you do next. **@purlsoho**

I use the Precious Metal Stitch Markers from **@cocoknits**. I saw *BLING* in the item description and didn't hesitate. They are gold-, silver-, and copper-covered steel and come in the cutest little box. Knitters deserve nice things.

Special shout-out to Felicia Eve, owner of String Thing Studio, my local yarn shop here in Brooklyn. Thank you for always having what I needed in a pinch, your cool vibes and suggestions. **@stringthingstudio**

When I use my 6-inch ruler from **@westknits** I always remember hanging out with Stephen at a bingo game knitting circle at Stephen & Penelope in Amsterdam, and our photo date in NYC. You inspire me, Stephen, in all your epicness.

flowers

My friend Kana, owner of Saffron Brooklyn, made the bouquet on page 4 especially for me. We went to the same art high school and reconnected as adults when I randomly strolled into her shop one day. These flowers are the concept images and acted as a color story for the book. I sent her color samples and said, "Just work your magic, it's guaranteed." When I walked into her shop, even among all the plants and arrangements, I spotted this baby immediately. I legit held back tears. This was mine; I just knew it! Saffron is a home away from home, an oasis, a muse. Buying ourselves flowers is definitely self-care. Thank you, Kana. **@saffronbk**

wardrobe

The ethically made and natural garments used in this 10×10 wardobe include pieces from: **@aliyawanek** **@nisoloshoes**

art

My Nature Nurture illustrations by Paula Champagne of **@makerchamp** brighten every cup of tea and plant-watering session. I see myself in the leaves, in her suns.

I've had my *Perks of a Library Card* print by Niki Dionne of **@actualfootageofme** for years. It's true to form and includes all my favorite colors and things to do.

muses and earth angels

I ate around a table with five siblings, and we all knew better than to save
our best for last. But my family, friends, supporters, and publishing team are
really the foundation of what made this work possible during a historic time.
Because of you, I did this! Thank you for your advice, your counsel, your
angel-like presence in all the ways we can show up to the work with ease and
faith and trust.

Adrienne, thank you for your tender love and unwavering patience. For turning on the light as I wrote in the same place from sunrise to sunset, for bringing me snacks. For handling your bouts of renovation fatigue like a champ
after several rearrangements and dual purposing of furniture past, present, and
future. You are my constant inspiration, my best friend. I love you so much.
My fairy really looked out when it brought me to you. To do life with you is
a blessing.

Mommy, Lamia, Tangier, Chrissy, Storm, my traveling companions, party
squad, and hype team. Thank you for not just telling me what I want to hear
and asking if I actually want that though in place of you just listening or pre-
tend listening to me rant, rave, and dream wilding with you. You have taught
me how to be a better communicator, a better person, a boundary maker, a
boundary keeper.

Jamila, when I texted you while making this book saying my writing felt dry
and crusty, you said, "Remember, you are a divine being for which only bril-
liance and creativity flows." Thank you for being you, for being such a beautiful friend and bright reflection.

To my editor, Meredith Clark, and the Abrams team, thank you for trusting in
my work and helping to bring this concept to life. I appreciate so much your
thoughtful surprise: picking fonts by Joshua Darden, the first known African
American type designer.

To my tech editor, Renee Lorion, your grounding and reassuring spirit was essential as I hopped from learning curve to learning curve centimeter by centimeter.

To my guides, whose work fuels endless possibility and who support me just by showing up and living in their truth: Audre Lorde, Octavia Butler, Toni Morrison, Alice Walker, Sojourner Truth, bell hooks, Maya Angelou, Angela Davis, Nikki Giovanni, Shirley Chisholm, Zora Neale Hurston, Alex Elle, Marlee Grace, Tricia Hersey, Michelle Obama, and so many others. I am forever grateful to you.

To my readers, thank you for joining me on this quest to live life joyously and honestly with knitting as a companion and teacher. My greatest hope is these patterns will guide, support, and encourage you to love yourself radically, all the parts of you, gently, every moment of every day. I love and appreciate you deeply.

With all my heart,

Brandi

about the author

My name is Brandi Cheyenne Harper. My pronouns are *she*, *her*, and *they*. Cancer sun, Pisces rising, Cancer moon. I get crabby without solitude. I'm loyal, I giggle a lot, and I love being home. My love language is just let me love on you, cook you nourishing meals you'll be surprised are vegetarian, and plan delicious surprises and treats for us. Maybe it's a bag of misty white peaches on a hot summer day. Maybe it's a giveaway. My ultimate goal is designing a life filled with and in tune with nature, simple and intricately constructed. To inspire people to build their most abundant and joyous lives, creatively and with ease.

The tools I make to empower have evolved over the years as I've explored my own strengths, learning curves, and passions. I write instructions for protective, futurist knits informed by Black, queer, and feminist theory. I've designed and taught crafty business classes. I earned degrees in vocal music, international politics, gender development, and French. I have certifications with the Anti-Violence Project (AVP) and the NYC Department of Health and Mental Hygiene. There was a time I felt like a wanderer, backpacking around the globe visiting yarn shops while learning a handful of words from different languages, cooking vegetables on different stoves.

When knitting begins to feel too much like work, I play in clay. I hand-build and throw on the potter's wheel, making nesting bowls and bud vases and structures to organize knitting tools and notions. Wholesome products supporting our ease and alignment. Moving into publishing is this wonderful opportunity to create tools encompassing all my passions. And to think, this is only the beginning.

index

A

abbreviations 32
ability 7, 8, 13, 101
about the author 156
access, *also see* privilege
   13, 14, 76
angelou, maya 137, 155
authenticity 8

B

balance 16, 109
beginning knitting 19–31
binding off 26, 42–45
   basic knit bind off 26,
   42, 66, 67, 68, 69, 70
   crochet bind off
   42, 81, 135
   3-needle bind
   off 42, 143
   i-cord bind off 43, 89,
   90, 91, 96, 99, 138
   tubular bind off 44,
   67, 68, 81
   knit hem bind off 45,
   107, 126
black lives matter 7
blocking 64, 99, 107, 115,
   127, 130, 149
black women 8, 14, 83, 93,
   117, 129, 145, 151
butler, octavia 101, 155

C

capitalism 7

casting on 33–39
   basic knit cast on
   double knit edge 35
   crochet chain provi-
   sional cast on 36
   i-cord cast on 38
   knit hem 37
   long tail cast on 33
   long tail tubular
   cast on 34
   thumb cast on 39
community 7, 8, 13, 73,
   101, 129, 145
courage 8, 11, 15
cowls 74, 100, 128, 140
creativity 7–11, 13,
   75–76, 93
crochet 8, 15, 36, 41, 42,
   58–59, 79–81, 84,
   104, 112
crochet seams 58–59,
   79–81, 104, 112

D

dawn cowl 100–107
decreases 46, 49–51
   K2TOG 49
   K3TOG 49
   P2TOG 49
   P3TOG 49
   SKP 50
   SK2P 50
   SKPP 50
   S2KP 51
diversity 14

E

edges, *see* casting on *as
   well as* selvedges
   applied i-cord edge 40
   reverse single crochet
   edging 41
elle, alex 141
essays
   allay 83
   audre 129–30
   aura 141
   dawn 101
   joie 109
   ode 117
   sojourn 93
   sola 137
   terran 145
   tombolo 75–76

F

fear 10, 11, 83, 129
finishing 60–64
fudging 15, 29
freedom 8, 93, 117

G

gauge 30–31, 65
giovanni, nikki 117

H

happiness 11, 108, 109, 141
hope 7, 10, 73, 101,
   109, 155

I

increases 32
  KFB 32, 49
  M1R 32, 46
  M1L 32, 46
  LLI 32, 47
  RLI 32, 47
  YO 32, 48
  BYO 32, 48
  KFB 32, 48

J

joy 11, 73, 108–109, 145,
  155, 156

K

knit stitch 22, 27, 29
knitwise 29

L

liberation 7, 10
lifestyle 13, 83
lorde, audre 7, 8, 11,
  129, 130
love 7, 8, 11, 73, 101,
  129, 141,

M

mock, janet 145,
modern guide to knitting,
  the framework 19–71
morrison, toni 8, 83

N

nature 16, 73, 76

O

ocean by the sea 28, 79,
  84, 102, 118, 147, 151

P

patterns 72–149
  cowls 79–81, 100–107,

128–135, 140–143
  hat 144–149
  mittens 108–114
  scarf 136–139
  shawl 92–99
  sweaters
    82–91, 116–127
pattern reading 29
passion 30, 75, 156
photography 151
power 7, 8, 10, 11, 13, 73,
  83, 109, 129, 130,
  141, 156
purl soho 20, 25, 64, 95,
  111, 133, 138, 143, 152
purl stitch 25, 29
purlwise 29
purpose 10, 30, 76, 129
practice 11, 14, 15, 16, 17,
  73, 101, 117
privilege, *also see*
  access 14

Q

queer 8, 145, 156

R

racism 7, 14, 83,
radical, *also see* self-care
  7, 8, 155
reddy, jamila 109, 117
representation 8, 14
revolutionary 8, 117, 130

S

seaming 60–63
  kitchener stitch 63
  mattress stitch 62
  seaming bind off to
  bind off 60
  seaming bind off to
  selvedge 61
seamless knitting 56–59

self-care, the princi-
  ples 13–17
selvedges, *also see* edging
  39, 40, 43, 61, 62,
  66, 67, 68
  i-cord selvedge 39
sewing, *see* seaming
short rows 51–55
  garter short rows 51
  german short rows 52
  wrap & turn short
  rows 53
  joining short rows 55
simone, nina 76
stitches
  garter stitch 22, 51, 66
  stockinette stitch
  25, 30, 66
  reverse stockinette 67
  1×1 rib 67
  brioche stitch 32,
  52, 68–69
  cables 70–71
  bloom stitch 65,
  145, 147

T

tools 13, 14, 28
truth, sojourner 93

U

unlearning 7–8

W

walker, alice 109
washing, *see* blocking
weaving in ends 27

Y

yarn 14, 16, 19, 28

Editor: Meredith A. Clark
Designer: Danielle Youngsmith
Managing Editor: Lisa Silverman
Production Manager: Kathleen Gaffney

Library of Congress Control Number: 2021932513

ISBN: 978-1-4197-4488-4
eISBN: 978-1-68335-923-4

Printed and bound in China
10 9 8 7 6 5 4 3 2 1

Abrams books are available at special discounts when purchased
in quantity for premiums and promotions as well as fundraising
or educational use. Special editions can also be created to
specification. For details, contact specialsales@abramsbooks.com
or the address below.

Abrams® is a registered trademark of Harry N. Abrams, Inc.

ABRAMS The Art of Books
195 Broadway, New York, NY 10007
abramsbooks.com